T0220254

Mastering GoLang

Mastering GoLang helps readers quickly understand the core concepts and then move on to practical projects using the Go programming language.

GoLang is often dubbed a game-changer in the world of programming languages. Instead of starting from scratch, Go was created using the C programming language. GoLang inherits C's disciplined grammar but with specific tweaks and enhancements to properly manage memory. This lessens the memory leakage problems that developers tend to face with C.

Go borrows and adapts notions from various programming languages while skipping characteristics that result in complicated, insecure, and unpredictable code. Go's concurrency features are well-suited to build the infrastructure for gigantic projects such as networking systems and distributed hardware. Go is also often employed in domains such as visuals, mobile applications, and Machine Learning.

Even though GoLang is a relatively new language, it has been adopted by several major organizations owing to its benefits such as code clarity, custom libraries, adaptability, multithreading, and a simple build process. Because Go is gaining traction in the development community, learning GoLang can open up new avenues across various fields and career trajectories.

Since it is still a relatively newer language, quality literature pertaining to Go is often hard to find. However, this particular book covers all the bases that you might need, and is an ideal companion for beginner-level developers looking to master Go programming.

With *Mastering GoLang*, learning GoLang becomes an easy task, and learners can use their skills to create innovative projects.

The *Mastering Computer Science* series is edited by Sufyan bin Uzayr, a writer and educator with over a decade of experience in the computing field.

Mastering Computer Science
Series Editor: Sufyan bin Uzayr

Mastering GoLang: A Beginner's Guide
Divya Sachdeva, D Nikitenko, and Aruqqa Khateib

Mastering GNOME: A Beginner's Guide
Jaskiran Kaur, Mathew Rooney, and Reza Nafim

Mastering Flutter: A Beginner's Guide
Divya Sachdeva, NT Ozman, and Reza Nafim

Mastering Vue.js: A Beginner's Guide
Lokesh Pancha, Divya Sachdeva, and Faruq KC

Mastering Rust: A Beginner's Guide
Divya Sachdeva, Faruq KC, and Aruqqa Khateib

Mastering Ubuntu: A Beginner's Guide
Jaskiran Kaur, Rubina Salafey, and Shahryar Raz

For more information about this series, please visit: https://www.routledge
.com/Mastering-Computer-Science/book-series/MCS

The "Mastering Computer Science" series of books are authored by the Zeba Academy team members, led by Sufyan bin Uzayr.

 Zeba Academy is an EdTech venture that develops courses and content for learners primarily in STEM fields, and offers education consulting to Universities and Institutions worldwide. For more info, please visit https://zeba.academy

Mastering GoLang
A Beginner's Guide

Edited by
Sufyan bin Uzayr

CRC Press
Taylor & Francis Group
Boca Raton London New York

CRC Press is an imprint of the
Taylor & Francis Group, an **informa** business

First Edition published 2023
by CRC Press
6000 Broken Sound Parkway NW, Suite 300, Boca Raton, FL 33487-2742

and by CRC Press
2 Park Square, Milton Park, Abingdon, Oxon, OX14 4RN

CRC Press is an imprint of Taylor & Francis Group, LLC

© 2023 Sufyan bin Uzayr

Library of Congress Cataloging-in-Publication Data

Names: Bin Uzayr, Sufyan, editor.
Title: Mastering GoLang : a beginner's guide / edited by Sufyan bin Uzayr.
Description: First edition. | Boca Raton : CRC Press, 2023. | Series: Mastering computer science series | Includes bibliographical references and index.
Identifiers: LCCN 2022021390 (print) | LCCN 2022021391 (ebook) |
ISBN 9781032315911 (hardback) | ISBN 9781032315904 (paperback) |
ISBN 9781003310457 (ebook)
Subjects: LCSH: Go (Computer program language)
Classification: LCC QA76.73.G63 M325 2023 (print) | LCC QA76.73.G63 (ebook) |
DDC 005.13/3--dc23/eng/20220802
LC record available at https://lccn.loc.gov/2022021390
LC ebook record available at https://lccn.loc.gov/2022021391

ISBN: 9781032315911 (hbk)
ISBN: 9781032315904 (pbk)
ISBN: 9781003310457 (ebk)

DOI: 10.1201/9781003310457

Typeset in Minion
by KnowledgeWorks Global Ltd.

Contents

Preface

The *Mastering Computer Science* covers a wide range of topics, spanning programming languages as well as modern-day technologies and frameworks. The series has a special focus on beginner-level content, and is presented in an easy-to-understand manner, comprising:

- Crystal-clear text, spanning various topics sorted by relevance,

- A special focus on practical exercises, with numerous code samples and programs,

- A guided approach to programming, with step-by-step tutorials for the absolute beginners,

- Keen emphasis on real-world utility of skills, thereby cutting the redundant and seldom-used concepts and focusing instead of industry-prevalent coding paradigm, and

- A wide range of references and resources to help both beginner and intermediate-level developers gain the most out of the books.

The *Mastering Computer Science* series starts from the core concepts, and then quickly moves on to industry-standard coding practices, to help learners gain efficient and crucial skills in as little time as possible. The books of the series assume no prior knowledge of coding, so even the absolute newbie coders can benefit from them.

The *Mastering Computer Science* series is edited by Sufyan bin Uzayr, a writer and educator with more than a decade of experience in the computing field.

About the Author

Sufyan bin Uzayr is a writer, coder, and entrepreneur with over a decade of experience in the industry. He has authored several books in the past, pertaining to a diverse range of topics, ranging from History to Computers/IT.

Sufyan is the Director of Parakozm, a multinational IT company specializing in EdTech solutions. He also runs Zeba Academy, an online learning and teaching vertical with a focus on STEM fields.

Sufyan specializes in a wide variety of technologies such as JavaScript, Dart, WordPress, Drupal, Linux, and Python. He holds multiple degrees, including ones in Management, IT, Literature, and Political Science.

Sufyan is a digital nomad, dividing his time between four countries. He has lived and taught in universities and educational institutions around the globe. Sufyan takes a keen interest in technology, politics, literature, history, and sports, and in his spare time, he enjoys teaching coding and English to young students.

Learn more at sufyanism.com

CHAPTER 1

Getting Started with Go

IN THIS CHAPTER

➤ Files and folders

➤ The terminal

➤ Text editors

Go is a general-purpose programming language created with systems programming in mind. It was invented in 2007 by Google's Robert Griesemer, Rob Pike, and Ken Thompson. It is strongly and statically typed, has built-in garbage collection support, and supports concurrent programming.

Packages are used to construct programs to manage dependencies efficiently. Go programming implementations employ a traditional compile and link model to generate executable binaries. The Go programming language was introduced in November 2009 and is currently used in some of Google's production systems.

GO PROGRAMMING FEATURES

- **Language Design:** The language's designers made a conscious decision to keep the language simple and easy to understand. The entire detailing is contained within a few pages, and some interesting design decisions were made using the language's Object-Oriented support. The language is opinionated, recommending a conversational method of

DOI: 10.1201/9781003310457-1

accomplishing things. Composition is preferred over Inheritance. The mantra in Go Language is "Do More with Less."

- **Package Management:** Go incorporates modern developer workflows for working with Open Source projects into managing external packages. Support for getting external packages and publishing our packages is provided directly in the tooling via a set of simple commands.

- **Powerful Standard Library:** Go has a robust standard library, distributed in the form of packages.

- **Static Typing:** Go is a language that is static typed. As a result, not only does this compiler work on successfully compiling code, but it also ensures type conversions and compatibility. Go avoids all of the issues we see in dynamically typed languages because of this feature.

- **Testing Support:** Go includes unit testing features by default, such as a simple mechanism for writing unit tests in parallel with our code, allowing us to understand code coverage through our tests. As an example, we can easily use this to generate code documentation.

- **Platform Independence:** Like the Java language, the Go Language supports platform independence. Because of its modular design and modularity, the code is compiled and converted into a binary form that is as small as possible, requiring no dependency. Its code can compile in any platform, server, or application on which we work.

WHY IS GoLang BETTER THAN THE OTHER PROGRAMMING LANGUAGES?

There is no respite for innovations and breakthroughs in the world of programming languages. Developers are constantly looking for a more straightforward, sophisticated, and project-friendly language. GoLang emerged as an amazing new programming language with a plethora of solutions. GoLang has taken the programming world by surprise since its introduction.

Many of the surprises that distinguish this language from others will be revealed here. Let's begin with an overview of the core capability in brief.

GoLang's Core Capability

Google developers reportedly conceived the GoLang while waiting for a code compilation project. This is why GoLang is the only language that combines all three desired features, namely ease of coding, efficient code compilation, and efficient execution. The fact that one can set all these capabilities together in a single language distinguishes GoLang from other programming languages.

Go, also known as GoLang, is a robust system-level language used for programming across large-scale network servers and large distributed systems. In simple words, through the context of what Google required for its network servers and distributed systems, GoLang emerged as an alternative to C++ and Java for app developers. The language was designed to eliminate the slowness and difficulties associated with programming for large and scalable servers and software systems. To be more specific, Go arrived at Google to provide the following solutions:

- Compilation and execution in a blink.
- Eliminating the need to work with different subsets of languages for a single project.
- Improved code readability and documentation.
- Providing an utterly consistent language.
- Allowing for simple program versioning.
- The ability to develop in multiple languages.
- Facilitating dependency management.

Multithreading and Concurrency

As hardware becomes more sophisticated over time, manufacturers add cores to the system to improve performance. When you come across with huge number of cores, the system must maintain database connections via microservices, manage queues, and maintain caches. This is why today's hardware requires a programming language that can better support concurrency and scale-up performance as the number of cores increases over time.

When working with multiple threads, most programming languages lack concurrent execution, which often slows down the pace of programming, compiling, and execution. This is where Go emerges as the most viable option for supporting both multithreading and concurrency.

When multi-core processors were widely available on sophisticated hardware, Go as a programming language came into existence. Naturally, the creators of Go placed a premium on concurrency. Go uses goroutines rather than threads, allowing it to handle many tasks simultaneously.

Go Empowers Hardware from Within

Because hardware processors only understand binaries, any application written in Java or JVM is interpreted into binaries. This interpretation at the hardware level increases the execution time. This is why compiled languages such as C/C++, which eliminate the step of understanding, can improve performance and speed of execution.

However, extracting and allocating variables in C/C++ involve a significant amount of complication and time. This is where Go shines as the ideal solution, combining the best of both worlds. Go, like C/C++, is a compiled language, which makes it as fast as they are. On the other hand, it uses garbage collection and object removal, just like Java, for variable allocation. As a result, Go is an ideal language for working within any hardware system.

The Unmatched Simplicity of Go

One of the primary benefits of adopting Go is its simplicity. Despite being a highly sophisticated language with a rich feature set, Go stands out from the group due to its simplicity and straightforward approach.

- **No Generics:** Generics or templates, which have long been a staple of various programming languages, often add to the obscurity and difficulty of understanding. By deciding to forego it, designers simplified things.

- **Single Executable:** GoLang does not include a runtime library. It can generate a single executable file that can be deployed simply by copying. This alleviates any concerns about making mistakes due to dependencies or version mismatches.

- **No Dynamic Libraries:** Go decided to forego any dynamic libraries to keep the language simple. However, in the latest Go 1.10 version, developers can upload dynamic libraries via plug-in packages. This has only been included as an added feature.

Inbuilt Testing and Profiling Framework

When developing a JavaScript application, many of us have encountered the complexities of selecting a testing framework through a series of analyses. The fact that we do not use more than 20% of the chosen framework most of the time is true. The same issue arises when good profiling is required for evaluation.

Go includes an inbuilt testing and profiling tool to help us test the application quickly and easily. Apart from providing ready-to-execute code examples, the tool can use for all types of testing and profiling needs.

Easy Learning Curve

One of the important advantages of Go is its low learning curve. We shouldn't be surprised if we say that all of GoLang's features can learn in just a few hours. Once we've mastered these fundamentals, we'll need to understand the best programming practices for specific needs as well as the standard library. However, a two- to three-hour session is sufficient to learn the language.

BEGINNING WITH Go

Several online IDEs, such as The Go Playground, repl.it, and others, can run Go programs without installing anything.

To install Go on our PCs or laptops, we will need the following two pieces of software: Text editor and Compiler.

Text Editor

A text editor provides a platform for us to write our source code. The following is a list of text editors:

- Windows notepad
- Brief
- OS Edit command
- Epsilon
- VS Code
- vm or vi
- Emacs

Finding a Go Compiler

The Go distribution is available as a binary installable for FreeBSD, Mac OS X, Linux, and Windows operating systems with 32-bit (386) and 64-bit (amd64) x86 processor architectures.

INSTALL Go ON WINDOWS

Before we begin, we must first install GoLang on our system. We need firsthand knowledge of what the Go Language is and what it does. Go is an open-source, statically typed programming language created in 2007 by Google's Robert Griesemer, Rob Pike, and Ken Thompson, but released in 2009. It also goes by the name GoLang and supports the procedural programming language. It was initially designed to boost programming productivity on large codebases, multi-core, and networked machines.

GoLang programs are easy to write. They can be written in any plain text editor such as notepad, notepad++, or something similar. One can also use an online IDE to write GoLang code or install one on their system to do writing and working on these codes easier. The best thing is that the IDE makes it easier to write the GoLang code because IDEs include many features such as an intuitive code editor, debugger, compiler, etc.

First, one must have the Go Language installed on their system to write GoLang Codes and perform various intriguing and valuable operations.

How Do We Determine the Go Language Version That Is Preinstalled?

Before we begin installing Go, it is good to check if it is already installed on our system. To see if our device has GoLang preinstalled, go to the command line (for Windows), search for cmd in the Run dialogue (+ R).

Execute following command:

```
go version
```

If GoLang is already installed on your PC, it will generate a message containing all of the GoLang version's details; otherwise, if GoLang is not installed on your PC, an error stating "Bad command or file name" will appear.

Downloading and Installing Go

Before we begin the installation procedure, we must first download it. All versions for Windows are available for download at https://go.dev/dl/.

Download GoLang for our system architecture and then follow the installation instructions for GoLang.

- **Step 1:** Unzip the downloaded archive file after it has been downloaded. After unzipping, we'll find a go folder in our current directory.

- **Step 2:** Copy and paste the extracted folder wherever we put it. In this case, we're installing it on the C drive.

- **Step 3:** Now, configure the environment variables. Right-click My PC and choose Properties. Select the Advanced System Settings from left menu and then Environment Variables.

- **Step 4:** From the system variables, select Path and then Edit. Then select New and enter the Path with bin directory where we pasted the Go folder. Here, we're going to change the path C:gobiC:\go\bin and click OK.

- **Step 5:** Create a new user variable that tells the Go command where the GoLang libraries are located. To do so, go to User Variables and select New.

Now enter GOROOT as the Variable name and the path to our GoLang folder as the Variable value. So, in this case, the Variable Value is C:\go\. After we've finished filling out the form, click OK.

Then, on Environment Variables, click OK, and our setup is complete. Now, check the GoLang version by typing go version into the command prompt.

After completing the installation process, any text editor or IDE can use to write GoLang Codes, which can then run on the IDE or the Command prompt using the command:

```
go run filename.go
```

WRITING THE FIRST Go PROGRAM

```
package main
import "fmt"
func main() {
      // print
      fmt.Println("Hello, everyone")
}
```

Explanation of Go program syntax:

- **Line 1:** contains the program's main package, including its overall content. It is the starting point for the program, so it must be written.

- **Line 2:** contains import "fmt," a preprocessor command that instructs the compiler to include the files in the package.

- **Line 3:** main function; this is the start of the program's execution.

- **Line 4:** fmt.

- **Println():** is a standard library function for printing something to the screen.

- **The fmt package:** has transmitted the Println method, which displays the output in this case.

- **Comments:** are used to explain code in the same way that they are in Java, C, or C++. Comment entries are ignored by compilers and are not executed. Comments can be single or multiple lines long.

Single-Line Comment

Syntax:

```
// single-line-comment
```

Multiline Comment

Syntax:

```
/* multiline-comment */
```

Example:
```
package main
import "fmt"
func main() {
    fmt.Println("2 + 2 =", 2 + 2)
}
```

Explanation of the Preceding Program

The preceding program uses the same package line, import line, function declaration, and Println function as the first Go program. Instead of printing the string "Hello, everyone," we print 2 + 2 = followed by the result of the expression 2 + 2. This expression comprises three parts: the int numeric literal 2, the + operator (which represents addition), and another int numeric literal 2.

Why Is There a "Go Language"?

Go is an attempt to combine the programming ease of an interpreted language and the safety of a statically typed, dynamically typed language with the efficiency of a compiled language. It also aspires to be cutting-edge, with networked and multi-core computing support.

What Is Absent in Go That Is Present in Other Languages?

- Go makes an effort to reduce typing in both senses of the word. Developers worked hard to keep clutter and complexity to a minimum throughout the design process.

- There are no forward declarations or header files; everything is only declared once.

- Simple type derivation using the := declare-and-initialize construct reduces stuttering.

- There is no type hierarchy: types simply exist; they are not required to announce their relationships.

Hardware Restrictions

We have observed that hardware and processing configuration change at a prolonged rate over a decade. In 2004, the P4 had a clock speed of 3.0 GHz. In 2018, the Macbook Pro has a clock speed of approximately (2.3 GHz vs. 2.66 GHz). We use more processors to speed up functionality, but the cost of using more processors also rises. As a result, we use limited processors, and with few processors, we have a heavy programming language whose threading consumes more memory and slows down our system's performance.

To address this issue, GoLang was designed so that instead of threading, it uses goroutine, which is similar to threading but consumes much less memory. Because threading consumes 1 MB of memory and goroutines 2 KB, it is easy to trigger millions of goroutines simultaneously. As a result of the points above, GoLang is a powerful language that handles concurrency in the same way that C++ and Java do.

Benefits and Drawbacks of the Go Language

Benefits:

- **Flexible:** It is adaptable because concise, straightforward, and simple to read.

- **Concurrency:** It allows multiple processes to run concurrently and effectively.

- **Quick Compilation:** Its compilation time is very short.

- **Library:** It includes an extensive standard library.

- Garbage collection is an essential feature of go. Go excels at providing a high level of control over memory allocation, and the garbage collector's latency has been dramatically reduced in recent versions.

- It checks for interface and type embedding.

Drawbacks:

- Even though many discussions about it, it does not support generics.

- Although the packages included with this programming language are pretty helpful, Go is not an object-oriented programming language in the traditional sense.

- Some libraries, particularly a UI toolkit, are missing.

Some popular Go Language applications include:

- **Docker:** It is a set of tools for managing and deploying Linux containers.

- **Red Hat:** It is Openshift and is a cloud computing platform as a service.

- **Kubernetes:** The Future of Seamlessly Automated Deployment.

- **Dropbox:** It shifted some of its critical components from Python to Go.

- **Netflix:** For two different aspects of their server architecture.

- **InfluxDB:** It is a time-series database that is open source and developed by InfluxData.

- **GoLang:** The language was created in Go.

TERMINAL

GoLand features an integrated terminal emulator that allows us to interact with our command-line shell from within the IDE. It may run Git commands, modify file permissions, and conduct other command-line functions without switching to a specialized terminal program.

The terminal emulator starts with our normal system shell, but it supports a variety of alternative shells, including Windows PowerShell, Command Prompt cmd.exe, sh, bash, zsh, csh, and others. See Configure the terminal emulator for further information on changing the shell.

The Open Terminal Tool Window

Select View | Tool Windows | Terminal from the main menu, or press Alt+F12.

By default, the terminal emulator runs with the current directory set to the current project's root directory.

Alternatively, we may right-click any file (for example, in the Project tool window or any open tab) and choose Open in Terminal from the context menu to launch the Terminal tool window with a new session in the file's directory.

Start New Session

Click Add button to create a new session in a new tab on the toolbar.

To run several sessions within a tab, right-click it and choose Split Right or Split Down from the context menu.

When we close the project or GoLand, the Terminal remembers tabs and sessions. Tab names, shell history, and the current working directory, are all saved.

Use the Terminal toolbar's Close button or right-click the tab and pick Close Tab from the context menu to close a tab.

To move between active tabs, press Alt+Right and Alt+Left. We may also press Alt+Down to get a list of all terminal tabs.

Right-click a tab and pick Rename Session from the context menu to rename it.

Ctrl+F will search for a specific string in a Terminal session. This searches the entire session's text, including the prompt, commands, and output.

Configure the terminal emulator as follows:

To open the IDE settings, press Ctrl+Alt+S and then select Tools | Terminal.

INSTALL Go ON MAC

Before we begin, we must first install GoLang on our system. We need firsthand knowledge of what the Go Language is and what it does. Go is an open-source, statically typed programming language created in

2007 by Google's Robert Griesemer, Rob Pike, and Ken Thompson but released in 2009. It also goes by the name GoLang and supports the procedural programming language. It was originally designed to boost programming productivity on large codebases, multi-core, and networked machines.

GoLang programs can be created in any plain text editor such as TextEdit, Sublime Text, or something similar. One can also use an online IDE to write GoLang code or install one on their system to make writing and working on these codes easier. For convenience, using an IDE makes it easier to write the GoLang code because IDEs include many features such as an intuitive code editor, debugger, compiler, etc.

The following are the steps for installing GoLang on MacOS:

- **Step 1:** Determine whether Go is installed or not. Before we begin installing Go, it is good to check to see if it is already installed on our system. To see if our device is preinstalled with GoLang, open the Terminal and type the following command:

```
go version
```

  If GoLang is already installed on your PC, it will generate a message with all of the GoLang version details available; otherwise, it will show an error.

- **Step 2:** Before we begin the installation process, we must first download it. As a result, all versions of Go for MacOS are available for download at https://go.dev/dl/.

  Download GoLang based on our system architecture. For the system, we have downloaded go1.13.1drawin-amd64.pkg.

- **Step 3:** Once the package has been downloaded, install it on our system.

- **Step 4:** Following the completion of the installation processes. Open Terminal (a command-line interface for MacOS) and use the GoLang version command to see if Go is installed correctly. It displays the GoLang version information, indicating that Go is successfully installed on our system.

After successfully installing Go on our system, we will now configure the Go workspace. A Go workspace is a folder on our computer that will house all of our Go code.

- **Step 1:** Make a folder called Go in our documents (or wherever we want in our system).

- **Step 2:** Tell the Go tools where to look for this folder. To begin, use the following command to navigate to our home directory:

```
cd ~
```

After that, use the following command to set the folder's path:

```
echo "export GOPATH=/Users/anki/Documents/go" >>
.bash_profile
```

In this case, we add export OPATH=/Users/anki/Documents/go to .bash_profile. The .bash profile file is automatically loaded when we log into our Mac account and contains all of our command-line interface startup configurations and preferences (CLI).

- **Step 3:** Run the following command to ensure that our .bash_profile contains the following path:

```
cat. bash_profile
```

- **Step 4:** Now, we'll use the following command to verify our go path. We can also skip this step if we prefer.

```
echo $GOPATH
```

Making Our First Program

- **Step 1:** Download and then install a text editor of your choice. Create a folder in Documents called Go (or whatever name we want) after installation (or wherever we want in our system). Create another folder called source in this folder and another folder called welcome in this source folder. All of our Go programs will save in this folder.

- **Step 2:** Let us write our first Go program. Open a text editor and type the Go program.

- **Step 3:** After creating the Go program, save it with the extension .go.

- **Step 4:** Launch the terminal to execute your first Go program.

- **Step 5:** Change the location of our program's files.

- **Step 6:** After changing directories, use the following command to run the Go program:

```
go run name_of_the_program.go
```

Execute a Go Program

Let's go over how to save the source code in a file, compile it, and then run the program. Please follow the instructions below:

- Open a text editor and paste the above code into it.

- Save the file with the name helloo.go

- Open the command prompt.

- Navigate to the location of saved file.

- Enter go run helloo.

- To run our code, go ahead and press enter.

- If your code is error-free, we will see "Hello Everyone" printed on the screen.

```
$ go run helloo.go
```

Hello, Everyone

Ascertain that the Go compiler is in our path and that it is running in the directory containing the source file helloo.go.

Do Programs in Go Link with the C/C++ Programming Language?

It is indeed possible to use C and Go in the same address space, but it is not a natural fit and may necessitate the use of special interface software. In addition, linking C code with Go code sacrifices Go's memory safety and stack management properties. Sometimes using C libraries to solve a problem is necessary, but doing so always introduces an element of risk that is not present in pure Go code, so proceed with caution.

If we must use C with Go, how you proceed is determined by the Go compiler implementation. The Go team provides support for three Go compiler implementations.

The default compiler is GC, followed by gccgo, which uses the GCC back end, and a slightly less mature gollvm, which uses the LLVM infrastructure.

Because gc has a different calling convention and linker than C, it cannot be called directly from C programs and vice versa. The cgo program implements a "foreign function interface" that allows Go code to call C libraries safely. This capability is extended to C++ libraries by SWIG.

Gccgo and gollvm can also be used with cgo and SWIG. Because they use a traditional API, it is possible to link code from these compilers directly with GCC/LLVM-compiled C or C++ programs with caution. However, doing so safely necessitates familiarity with all languages' calling conventions and consideration for stack limits when calling C or C++ from Go.

IN GoLang, HOW DO WE CREATE AN EMPTY FILE?

Go Language, like other computer languages, allows us to construct files. It offers the Create() function for creating a file, which is used to create or truncate the given named file.

If the specified file already exists, then this method will truncate it.

If a specified file does not exist, this method will create one with mode 0666.

This procedure will return a *PathError exception if the specified path is incorrect.

This function returns a file descriptor that may be read and written.

Because it is specified in the os package, we must import the os package in our program to use the Create() method.

Syntax:

```
func Create(file-name string) (*File, error)
```

First example:

```
package main
import (
    "log"
    "os"
)
func main() {
    // empty file Creation
    // Create() function Using
    myfile, es := os.Create("helloo.txt")
    if es != nil {
        log.Fatal(es)
    }
```

```
    log.Println(myfile)
    myfile.Close()
}
```

Second example:

```
package main
import (
    "log"
    "os"
)
func main() {
    // empty file Creation
    // Create() function Using
    myfile, es := os.Create("/Users/anki/
Documents/new_folder/helloo.txt")
    if es != nil {
        log.Fatal(es)
    }
    log.Println(myfile)
    myfile.Close()
}
```

In GoLang, We May Check Whether a Given File Exists or Not

The IsNotExist() function in the Go programming language allows us to
determine if a given file exists or not. If the above-mentioned function
returns true, then the error is known to report that the specified file or
directory does not already exist, and if it returns false, it means that the
supplied file or directory does exist. ErrNotExist and several syscall errors
also satisfy this procedure. Because it is specified in the os package, we must
import the os package in our program to use the IsNotExist() method.

Syntax:

```
func IsNotExist(es error) bool
```

First example:

```
package main
import (
    "log"
    "os"
```

```go
)
var (
    myfile *os.FileInfo
    es  error
)
func main() {
    // Stat() function returns the file info and
    //if there is no file, then it will return
error
    myfile, es := os.Stat("helloo.txt")
    if es != nil {
      // Checking if given file exists or not
      // Using the IsNotExist() function
        if os.IsNotExist(es) {
            log.Fatal("File not Found")
        }
    }
    log.Println("File Exist")
    log.Println("File Detail is:")
    log.Println("Name is: ", myfile.Name())
    log.Println("Size is: ", myfile.Size())
}
```

Second example:

```go
package main

import (
    "log"
    "os"
)
var (
    myfile *os.FileInfo
    es  error
)
func main() {
    // Stat() function returns the file info and
    // if there is no file, then it will return
error
    myfile, es := os.Stat("/Users/anki/Documents/
new_folder/myfolder/helloo.txt")
    if es != nil {
      // Checking if given file exists or not
```

```go
        // Using IsNotExist() function
        if os.IsNotExist(es) {
            log.Fatal("File not Found")
        }
    }
    log.Println("File Exist")
    log.Println("File Detail is:")
    log.Println("Name is: ", myfile.Name())
    log.Println("Size is: ", myfile.Size())
}
```

CREATE A DIRECTORY IN Go

In Go, use the os.Mkdir() method to create a single directory. Use os.MkdirAll() to establish a folder hierarchy (nested directories). Both methods need a path and the folder's permission bits as parameters.

Make a Single Directory

```go
package main
import (
    "log"
    "os"
)
func main() {
    if er := os.Mkdir("a", os.ModePerm); er != nil {
        log.Fatal(er)
    }
}
```

Make a Directory Hierarchy (Nested Directories)

```go
package main
import (
    "log"
    "os"
)
func main() {
    if er := os.MkdirAll("a/b/c/d", os.ModePerm); er
!= nil {
        log.Fatal(er)
    }
}
```

The os.Mkdir() function generates a new directory with the specified name but does not allow for the creation of subdirectories.

In this chapter, we covered the introduction of Go with its features, advantages, and disadvantages. We also covered Go installation in Windows and Mac. Moreover, we covered Files and Folders, The Terminal, and Text Editors.

CHAPTER 2

GoLang Tools

IN THIS CHAPTER

➢ How to Read a Go Program

In Chapter 1, we covered the introduction of Go along with its advantages and disadvantages. We also covered Go installation, Files and Folders, Terminal, and Text Editors. This chapter will discuss how to read and write a program.

HOW TO READ AND WRITE PROGRAMS IN Go

GoLang includes an extensive built-in library that may use to conduct file read and write operations. The io/ioutil module is all about reading from files on the local system. One can use the io/ioutil module to save data to a file.

The fmt module supports formatted I/O by providing methods for reading input from stdin and printing output to stdout. The log module is a basic logging package that is implemented.

It introduces a Logger type with methods for formatting output. The os module allows us to use native operating-system functions. Buffered I/O is implemented by the bufio module, which helps to enhance CPU speed.

- **os.Create()**: This function creates a file with the specified name. If another file with the same name already exists, the create method truncates it.

DOI: 10.1201/9781003310457-2

- **ioutil.ReadFile():** The only parameter to the ioutil.ReadFile() function is the path to the file to be read. This procedure either returns the file's contents or an error.

- **ioutil.WriteFile():** It returns the ioutil. WriteFile() is a function used to save data to a file. The WriteFile() function accepts three parameters: the location of the file to which we want to write, the data object, and the FileMode, which contains the file's mode and permission bits.log.

- **Fatalf:** Fatalf will terminate the application after printing the log message. It is similar to doing Printf() followed by os.Exit (1).

- **log.Panicf:** Panic is similar to an exception that may occur during runtime. Panicln is the same as Println() followed by a panic() call. The parameter supplied to panic() is displayed when the program exits.

- **bufio.NewReader(os.Stdin):** This function returns a new Reader with the default buffer size (4096 bytes).

- **inputReader.ReadString('n'):** This method reads user input from stdin until the first occurrence of a delimiter in the input and returns a string containing the data up to and including the delimiter. An error before locating a delimiter provides the data read before the fault and the error itself.

First example: For best results, use the offline compiler. Save the file as a .go file. To run the program, follow-up the below given command.

```
go run file-name.go

// program to read and write files
package main
// importing packages
import (
    "fmt"
    "io/ioutil"
    "log"
    "os"
)
func CreateFile() {
    // fmt package implements formatted I/O, it
has functions like Printf and Scanf
```

```go
    fmt.Printf("Writing file in Go lang\n")
    // in case error is thrown it is received by
err variable and Fatalf method of
    // log prints error message and stops program
execution
    file, er := os.Create("test1.txt")
    if er != nil {
        log.Fatalf("failed creating file: %s", er)
    }
    // Defer is used for the purposes of cleanup
like closing a running file after the file has
    // been written and the main function has
completed execution
    defer file.Close()
    // len variable captures the length of string
written to the file.
    len, er := file.WriteString("Welcome
Everyone"+
            " Program demonstrates reading and
writing"+
                    " operations to a file in
the Go lang.")
    if er != nil {
        log.Fatalf("failed writing to file: %s", er)
    }
    // Name() method returns name of the file as
presented to Create() method.
    fmt.Printf("\nFile Name: %s", file.Name())
    fmt.Printf("\nLength: %d bytes", len)
}
func ReadFile() {
    fmt.Printf("\n\nReading a file in the Go
lang\n")
    fileName := "test1.txt"
    // The ioutil package contains inbuilt
    // methods like ReadFile that reads
    // filename and returns contents.
    data, er := ioutil.ReadFile("test.txt")
    if er != nil {
        log.Panicf("failed reading data from file:
%s", er)
    }
    fmt.Printf("\nFile Name is: %s", fileName)
```

```
    fmt.Printf("\nSize is: %d bytes", len(data))
    fmt.Printf("\nData is: %s", data)
}
// main function
func main() {
    CreateFile()
    ReadFile()
}
```

Second example: GoLang program code reads and writes files based on user input.

```
// Program to read and write files
package main
// importing requires packages
import (
    "bufio"
    "fmt"
    "io/ioutil"
    "log"
    "os"
)
func CreateFile(filename, text string)
{
    // fmt package implements formatted I/O
    // and contains the inbuilt methods like the
Printf and Scanf
    fmt.Printf("Writing to a file in the Go
lang\n")

    // Creating file using Create() method with
user inputted filename and err
    // variable catches any error thrown
    file, er := os.Create(filename)

    if er != nil {
        log.Fatalf("failed creating file: %s", er)
    }
    // closing running file after the main method
has completed execution and
    // writing to the file is complete
    defer file.Close()
```

```go
    // writing data to file using
    // WriteString() method and
    // length of the string is stored in the len
variable
    len, er := file.WriteString(text)
    if er != nil {
        log.Fatalf("failed writing to file: %s",
er)
    }
    fmt.Printf("\nFile Name is: %s", file.Name())
    fmt.Printf("\nLength is: %d bytes", len)
}
func ReadFile(filename string) {
    fmt.Printf("\n\nReading a file in the Go
lang\n")
    // file is read using ReadFile() method of the
ioutil package
    data, err := ioutil.ReadFile(filename)
    // in case of an error
    // the error statement is printed, program is
stopped
    if er != nil {
        log.Panicf("failed reading data from file:
%s", er)
    }
    fmt.Printf("\nFile Name is: %s", filename)
    fmt.Printf("\nSize is: %d bytes", len(data))
    fmt.Printf("\nData is: %s", data)
}
// main function
func main() {
    // user input for the filename
    fmt.Println("Enter-filename: ")
    var filename string
    fmt.Scanln(&filename)
    // user input for the file content
    fmt.Println("Enter-text: ")
    inputReader := bufio.NewReader(os.Stdin)
    input, _ := inputReader.ReadString('\n')
    // file is created then read
    CreateFile(filename, input)
    ReadFile(filename)
}
```

IN GoLang, HOW TO RENAME AND MOVE A FILE

The Rename() function in the Go programming language allows us to rename and transfer an existing file to a new directory. This procedure is used to rename and transfer a file from one path to another.

If the specified new path already exists and is not in a directory, this procedure will overwrite it. However, OS-specific limitations may apply if the specified old and new paths are in separate directories.

If the specified path is wrong, type *LinkError will throw an error.

Because it is specified in the os package, we must import the os package in our program to use the Remove() method.

Syntax:

```
func Rename(old-path, new-path string) error
```

First example:

```
// Program to illustrate how to rename,
// move a file in the default directory
package main
import (
    "log"
    "os"
)
func main() {
    // Rename and Remove a file
    // Using Rename() function
    OriginalPath := "helloo.txt"
    NewPath := "abc.txt"
    es := os.Rename(Original_Path, New_Path)
    if es != nil {
        log.Fatal(es)
    }

}
```

Second example:

```
// Program to illustrate how to rename,
//remove a file in new directory
package main
```

```
import (
    "log"
    "os"
)
func main() {
    // Rename and Remove file
    // Using Rename() function
    OriginalPath := "/Users/anki/Documents/new_
folder/helloo.txt"
    NewPath := "/Users/anki/Documents/new_folder/
myfolder/abc.txt"
    es := os.Rename(OriginalPath, NewPath)
    if es != nil {
        log.Fatal(es)
    }
}
```

HOW TO READ FILES LINE BY LINE TO STRING

The bufio package Scanner is used to read a file line by line. Let the text file be called sample1.txt, and the content inside the file is as follows.

The Go programming language is an open-source, statically compiled programming language. Rob Pike, Ken Thompson, and Robert Grieserner created it at Google. It is sometimes referred to as GoLang. The Go programming language is a general-purpose programming language designed to develop large-scale, complicated software.

```
package main
import (
    "bufio"
    "fmt"
    "log"
    "os"
)
func main() {
    // os.Open() opens specific file in the
    // read-only mode,
    // this return pointer of type os.
    file, er := os.Open("sample1.txt")

    if er != nil {
        log.Fatalf("failed to open")
```

```
    }
    // bufio.NewScanner() function is called in which
    // object os.File passed as its parameter
    // this returns object bufio.Scanner which is used
on the
    // bufio.Scanner.Split() method
    scanner := bufio.NewScanner(file)
    // The bufio.ScanLines is used as
    // input to method bufio.Scanner.Split()
    // and then scanning forwards to each
    // new line using bufio.Scanner.Scan() method.
    scanner.Split(bufio.ScanLines)
    var text []string
    for scanner.Scan() {
        text = append(text, scanner.Text())
    }
    // The method os.File.Close() is called
    // on the os.File object to close file
    file.Close()
      // and then a loop iterates through,
    // prints each of the slice values.
    for _, each_ln := range text {
        fmt.Println(each_ln)
    }
}
```

This chapter covered how to read and write Go programs, read a file line by line to string, and how to rename files.

CHAPTER 3

Data Types

IN THIS CHAPTER

> ➤ Numbers

> ➤ Booleans

> ➤ Strings

In Chapter 2, we discussed on how to read the file in Go and how to rename the file. In this chapter, we will wrap numbers, Booleans, and strings.

BASIC SYNTAX

In Chapter 2, we explored the fundamental structure of a Go program. The other essential building parts of the Go programming language will be much easier to grasp now.

Tokens

A Go program is made up of different tokens. Tokens can be keywords, identifiers, constants, string literals, or symbols. For instance, the following Go statement is made up of six tokens:

```
fmt.Println("Hello, Everyone")
```

Individual tokens are as follows:

```
fmt
```

```
.
```

```
Println
```

DOI: 10.1201/9781003310457-3

```
(
    "Hello, Everyone"
)
```

Line Separator

The line separator key is a statement terminator in a Go program. Individual statements, in other words, do not require a particular separator like ";" in C. The Go compiler uses the statement terminator ";" to signify the end of one logical entity.

Take a look at the following statements, for example:

```
fmt.Println("Hello, Everyone")
fmt.Println("We are in the world of Go Programming")
```

Comments

Comments are similar to help messages in our Go program, and the compiler ignores them. They begin with/* and end with the characters */, as illustrated below.

```
/* My first Go program */
```

There can be no comments within comments, and they do not appear within strings or characters literal.

Identifiers

A Go identifier identifies a variable, function, or other user-defined entity. An identifier begins with a letter A to Z, a to z, or an underscore. It can be followed by underscores, zero or more letters, or digits.

```
identifier = letter { letter | unicode_digit }
```

Punctuation characters such as @, $, and percent are not permitted within identifiers in Go. Go is a case-sensitive computer language. Thus, in Go, Manpower and manpower are two distinct identities. The following are some instances of appropriate identifiers:

```
ramesh      sehgal    xyz    move_name    x_123
myname40    _temp     j      x23b8        retVal
```

Keywords are not permitted to be used as identifiers.

Identifier _ is a unique identifier, sometimes known as a blank identifier.

We will later discover that all types, variables, constants, labels, package names, and package import names must be identifiers.

An exported identifier begins with a Unicode upper case letter. In many other languages, the word exported can be translated as public. Non-exported identifiers do not begin with a Unicode upper case letter. The term "non-exported" can be understood as "private in several different languages." Eastern characters are now categorized as non-exported letters. Non-exported IDs are sometimes known as unexported identifiers.

Here are some examples of legally exported identifiers:

```
Player_7
DidSomething
VERSION
Ĝo
Π
```

Here are some examples of legal non-exported identifiers:

```
_
_status
memeStat
books
π
```

Here are some examples of tokens that are not permitted to be used as identifiers:

```
// Starting with Unicode digit.
321
4apples
// Containing the Unicode characters not
// satisfying requirements.
c.d
*ptr
$names
c@d.e
// These are keywords.
type
range
```

Keywords

The reserved terms in Go are listed in the following table. These reserved terms are not permitted to be used as constants, variables, or other identifiers.

case	default	import	interface	struct
chan	defer	go	map	select
break	else	if	package	type
const	fallthrough	goto	range	switch
continue	for	func	return	var

They are divided into six categories: const, func, import, package, type, and var are used to declare various types of code components in Go programs.

Some composite type denotations use chan, interface, map, and struct as components.

To manage the code flow, break, case, continue, default, otherwise, fallthrough, for, goto, if, range, return, select, and switch are used.

Both defer and go control flow terms, although in different ways.

Whitespace

In Go, whitespace refers to blanks, tabs, newline characters, and comments. A blank line has simply whitespace, maybe with a remark, and is entirely ignored by the Go compiler.

Whitespaces divides one section of a statement from another and allows the compiler to determine where one element, int, ends, and the next element begins in a statement. As a result, in the following statement:

```
var ages int;
```

For the compiler to distinguish between int and ages, there must be at least one whitespace character (typically a space). In contrast, consider the following statement:

```
fruits = grapes + oranges;  // get the total amount of
fruit
```

There are no whitespace characters required between fruit and =, or between = and grapes; however, we are welcome to include any for readability purposes.

DATA TYPES IN Go

Data types define the sorts of data stored in a valid Go variable. The type is separated into four types in the Go language, which are as follows:

- Numbers, strings, and Booleans are examples of basic types.

- Arrays and structs are examples of aggregate types.

- Pointers, slices, maps, functions, and channels are examples of reference types.

- Interface type.

This section will go through Basic Data Types in the Go programming language. The Basic Data Types are further divided into three subcategories, which are as follows:

- Numbers

- Booleans

- Strings

Numbers

Numbers in Go are separated into three subcategories, which are as follows:

- **Integers:** The Go language supports both signed and unsigned integers in four distinct sizes, as indicated in the following table. The signed integer is denoted by int, whereas the unsigned integer is denoted by uint.

Data Type	Description
int8	8 bit signed integer
int16	16 bit signed integer
int32	32 bit signed integer
int64	64 bit signed integer
uint8	8 bit unsigned integer
uint16	16 bit unsigned integer
uint32	32 bit unsigned integer
uint64	64 bit unsigned integer
Int	In and uint have the same size, either 32 or 64 bits
uint	In and uint have the same size, either 32 or 64 bits
Rune	It is the same as int32 and represents Unicode code points
Byte	It is an abbreviation for uint8
Uintptr	It is a type of unsigned integer. It has no fixed width, but it can store all of the bits of a pointer value

Example:

```
// Program to illustrate the use of integers
package main
import "fmt"
func main() {
    // 8-bit unsigned int using
    var A uint8 = 225
    fmt.Println(A, A-3)
    // Using 16-bit signed int
    var B int16 = 32767
    fmt.Println(B+2, B-2)
}
```

Floating Point Numbers

In Go, floating-point numbers are classified into two types, as illustrated in the following table:

Data Type	Description
float32	32 bit IEEE 754 floating point number
float64	64 bit IEEE 754 floating point number

Example:

```
// I illustrate the use of floating-point numbers
package main
import "fmt"
func main()
{
    x := 22.46
    y := 35.88
    // Subtract of two floating-point number
    z := y-x
    // Display result
    fmt.Printf("Result is: %f", z)
    // Display type of c variable
    fmt.Printf("\nThe type of z is : %T", z)
}
```

Complex Numbers

The complex numbers are separated into two portions in the following table. These complex integers also include float32 and float64. The built-in function generates a complex number from its imaginary and real components, while the built-in imaginary and real functions remove those components.

Data Type	Description
complex64	Complex numbers with float32 as both a real and imaginary component.
complex128	Complex numbers with float64 as both a real and imaginary component.

Example:

```
// Illustrate the use of complex numbers
package main
import "fmt"
func main() {
    var x complex128 = complex(7, 3)
    var y complex64 = complex(8, 3)
    fmt.Println(x)
    fmt.Println(y)
    // Display type
    fmt.Printf("The type of x is %T and "+
            "the type of y is %T", x, y)
}
```

Booleans

The Boolean data type merely represents one bit of information: true or false. The values of type Boolean are not inherently or explicitly transformed to any other type.

Example:

```
// Program to illustrate the use of booleans
package main
import "fmt"
func main() {
    // variables
    strg1 := "PeeksofPeeks"
    strg2:= "peeksofpeeks"
    strg3:= "PeeksofPeeks"
    results1:= strg1 == strg2
    results2:= strg1 == strg3
        // Display result
    fmt.Println( results1)
```

```
    fmt.Println( results2)
    // Display type of
    // results1 and results2
    fmt.Printf("The type of results1 is %T and "+
                 "the type of results2 is %T",
                            results1, results2)

}
```

Strings

A string data type is a series of Unicode code points. In other terms, a string is a series of immutable bytes, which implies that once a string is created, it cannot change. A string can include any data in human-readable form, including zero value bytes.

Example:

```
// Program to illustrate the use of strings
package main
import "fmt"
func main()
{
    // strf variable stores strings
    strg := "PeeksofPeeks"
    // Display length of the string
    fmt.Printf("Length of the string is:%d",
                                len(strg))
    // Display string
    fmt.Printf("\nString is: %s", strg)
    // Display type of strg variable
    fmt.Printf("\nType of strg is: %T", strg)
}
```

This chapter covered numbers, Booleans, and strings with its relevant examples.

CHAPTER 4

Variables and Constants

IN THIS CHAPTER

> Variables in Go

> Constants

> Variable scope in Go

> Declaration of multiple variables

In Chapter 3, we covered numbers, strings, and Booleans. In this chapter, we will cover variables, scope, and constants.

VARIABLES IN Go

A typical program employs a variety of variables that may change during execution. For instance, consider a program that runs various operations on the values entered by the user. The values submitted by one user may differ from those entered by another. As a result, variables are required. It is because another user may not utilize the same values again.

When a user enters a new value in the process of operation that will utilize further, they can store it temporarily in the computer's Random Access Memory, and the values in this area of memory fluctuate throughout the execution, giving rise to another word for this, which is known as Variables. So, in essence, a Variable is a placeholder for information that may update at runtime. Variables enable the retrieval and manipulation of stored data.

DOI: 10.1201/9781003310457-4

Variable Naming Guidelines:

- Always begin the variable name with a letter or underscore (_). In addition, the letters "a-z" or "A-Z" or the digits 0–9 and the character "_" may appear in the names.
  Peeks peeks, _peeks24 // valid-variable
  124Peeks, 24peeks   // invalid-variable

- Never begin any variable name with a digit.
  235peeks // illegal-variable

- The variable's name is case-sensitive.
  peeks and Peeks are the two different variables

- Keywords are not permitted to be used as variable names.

- There is no restriction to the length of the variable's name; however, it is recommended to be no more than 4–15 letters long.

Declaring a Variable

Variables in the Go programming language may declare in the following two ways.

Using the var Keyword

Variables in Go are created using the var keyword of a particular type, linked with a name, and given an initial value.

Syntax:

```
var variable_name type = expression
```

Important Notes:

- In the preceding syntax, either the type or the = expression can delete, but not both, in the definition of a variable.

- If the type is deleted, the value-initialize in the expression determines the type of the variable.

Example:

```
// Illustrate the concept of variable
package main
  import "fmt"
```

```go
func main() {
// Variable declared &
// initialized without the explicit type
var myvariable1 = 30
var myvariable2 = "PeeksofPeeks"
var myvariable3 = 37.80
// Display value and
// type of the variables
fmt.Printf("Value of myvariable1 is : %d\n",
                                myvariable1)
fmt.Printf("Type of myvariable1 is : %T\n",
                                myvariable1)
fmt.Printf("Value of myvariable2 is : %s\n",
                                 myvariable2)
fmt.Printf("Type of myvariable2 is : %T\n",
                                myvariable2)
fmt.Printf("Value of myvariable3 is : %f\n",
                                myvariable3)
fmt.Printf("Type of myvariable3 is : %T\n",
                                myvariable3)

}
```

- If the expression is deleted, the variable will have a zero value for the type, such as zero for numbers, false for Booleans, "" for strings, and nil for interface and reference types. As a result, there is no idea of an uninitialized variable in the Go programming language.

Example:

```go
// Program to illustrate the concept of variable
package main
import "fmt"
    func main() {
    // Variable declared &
    // initialized without the expression
    var myvariable1 int
    var myvariable2 string
    var myvariable3 float64
    // Display zero-value of the variables
    fmt.Printf("Value of myvariable1 is : %d\n",
                                    myvariable1)
    fmt.Printf("Value of myvariable2 is : %s\n",
                                    myvariable2)
```

```
        fmt.Printf("Value of myvariable3 is : %f",
                                        myvariable3)
}
```

- We may define several variables of the same type in a single declaration when using type.

Example:

```
// Program to illustrate
// the concept of variable
package main
import "fmt"
func main() {
    // Multiple variables of same type
    // are declared & initialized in single line
    var myvariable1, myvariable2, myvariable3 int
= 4, 554, 68
    // Display values of the variables
    fmt.Printf("Value of myvariable1 is : %d\n",
                                        myvariable1)
    fmt.Printf("Value of myvariable2 is : %d\n",
                                        myvariable2)
    fmt.Printf("Value of myvariable3 is : %d",
                                        myvariable3)
}
```

- If we remove the type, we can define many variables of various types in a single declaration. The initialized values indicate the type of variable.

Example:

```
// Program to illustrate
// the concept of variable
package main
import "fmt"
func main() {
// Multiple variables of different types
// are declared and initialized in single line
```

```
var myvariable1, myvariable2, myvariable3 = 4,
"CFG", 69.56
// Display value &
// type of variables
fmt.Printf("Value of myvariable1 is : %d\n",
                                    myvariable1)
fmt.Printf("Type of myvariable1 is : %T\n",
                                    myvariable1)
fmt.Printf("\nValue of the myvariable2 is : %s\n",
                                    myvariable2)
fmt.Printf("Type of the myvariable2 is : %T\n",
                                    myvariable2)

fmt.Printf("\nThe value of the myvariable3 is :
%f\n",
                                    myvariable3)
fmt.Printf("Type of the myvariable3 is : %T\n",
                                    myvariable3)
}
```

- The calling function that returns multiple values allows us to initialize a set of variables.

Example:

```
// Here, os.Open function return a
// file in x variable and an error
// in y variable
var x, y = os.Open(name)
```

Using the Short Variable Declaration

Short variable declaration is used to define and initialize local variables in functions.

Syntax:

```
variable-name:= expression
```

Note: Please do not mix up := and =, as := is a declaration while = is an assignment.

Important Notes:

- The type of the expression decides the type of the variable in the preceding expression.

Example:

```
// Program to illustrate
// the concept of variable
package main
import "fmt"
func main()
{
// Using short-variable declaration
myvar1 := 37
myvar2 := "PeeksofPeeks"
myvar3 := 36.63
// Display value and type of the variables
fmt.Printf("Value of myvar1 is : %d\n", myvar1)
fmt.Printf("Type of myvar1 is : %T\n", myvar1)
fmt.Printf("\nValue of myvar2 is : %s\n", myvar2)
fmt.Printf("Type of myvar2 is : %T\n", myvar2)
fmt.Printf("\nValue of myvar3 is : %f\n", myvar3)
fmt.Printf("Type of myvar3 is : %T\n", myvar3)
}
```

- Because of their brevity and versatility, most local variables are defined and initialized using short variable declarations.

- Variables with the var declaration are used for local variables that need an explicit type that differs from the initializer expression or variables whose values are assigned later, and the initialized value is irrelevant.

- When using a short variable declaration, we can declare several variables in a single declaration.

Example:

```
// Go program to illustrate
// concept of variable
package main
import "fmt"
func main()
```

```
{
// Using short variable declaration
// Multiple variables of the same types
// are declared & initialized in single line
myvar1, myvar2, myvar3 := 830, 44, 66
// Display value and
// type of variables
fmt.Printf("Value of myvar1 is : %d\n", myvar1)
fmt.Printf("Type of myvar1 is : %T\n", myvar1)
fmt.Printf("\nValue of myvar2 is : %d\n", myvar2)
fmt.Printf("Type of myvar2 is : %T\n", myvar2)
fmt.Printf("\nValue of myvar3 is : %d\n", myvar3)
fmt.Printf("Type of myvar3 is : %T\n", myvar3)
}
```

- The calling function can initialize a group of variables that return multiple values in a short variable declaration.

Example:

```
// os.Open function return
// a file in x variable and an
// error in y variable
x, y := os.Open(name)
```

- A short variable declaration behaves similarly to an assignment only when referring to previously defined variables in the same lexical block. Variable declarations in the outer block are ignored. And, as shown in the following example, at least one variable is a new variable created from these two variables.

Example:

```
// Program to illustrate
// the concept of variable
package main
import "fmt"
func main() {
// Using the short variable declaration
// short variable declaration acts
// as an assignment for the myvar2 variable
// because same variable present in same block
```

```
// so the value of myvar2 is changed from 55 to 100
myvar1, myvar2 := 39, 55
myvar3, myvar2 := 55, 100
// If we try to run the commented lines,
// then compiler will gives the error because
// these variables are already defined
// myvar1, myvar2 := 53, 57
// myvar2:= 210
// Display the values of the variables
fmt.Printf("Value of myvar1 and myvar2 is : %d
%d\n",

myvar1, myvar2)
fmt.Printf("Value of myvar3 and myvar2 is : %d
%d\n",

myvar3, myvar2)
}
```

- We can define numerous variables of various kinds in a single declaration using a short variable declaration. The expression determines the type of these variables.

Example:

```
// Program to illustrate
// the concept of variable
package main
import "fmt"
func main() {
// Using the short variable declaration
// Multiple variables of the different types
// are declared and initialized in single line
myvar1, myvar2, myvar3 := 700, "Peeks", 48.56
// Display value and type of the variables
fmt.Printf("Value of myvar1 is : %d\n", myvar1)
fmt.Printf("Type of myvar1 is : %T\n", myvar1)
fmt.Printf("\nValue of myvar2 is : %s\n", myvar2)
fmt.Printf("Type of myvar2 is : %T\n", myvar2)
fmt.Printf("\nValue of myvar3 is : %f\n", myvar3)
fmt.Printf("Type of myvar3 is : %T\n", myvar3)
}
```

CONSTANTS

As the word CONSTANT implies, it is fixed; similarly, in programming languages, once the value of a constant is declared, it cannot change further. Constants can be any fundamental data kind, such as an integer constant, a floating constant, a character constant, or a literal string.

How Should We Declare?

Constants are defined similarly to variables, but with the const keyword as a prefix to specify a constant of a specified type. It is not possible to describe it using the := syntax.

Example:

```
package main

import "fmt"
const Pi = 3.14
func main()
{
    const POP = "PeeksofPeeks"
    fmt.Println("Hello", world)
    fmt.Println("Happy", Pi, "Day")
    const Correct= true
    fmt.Println("Go rules?", Correct)
}
```

Untyped and Typed Numeric Constants

Typed constants behave like immutable variables and can only interact with variables of the same type, but untyped constants behave like literals and interact with similar variables. In Go, constants can specify with or without a type. The following is an example of typed and untyped numeric constants, both named and nameless.

```
const untypedInteger = 321
const untypedFloating typed = 321.12
const typedInteger int = 321
const typedFloatingPoint float64 = 321.12
```

The following is a list of Go Language constants:

- Numeric Constant (Integer constant, Floating constant, and Complex constant)

- Boolean Constant

- String Literals

Numeric Constant

Numeric constants are values with high precision. Because Go is a statically typed language, operations that combine numeric types are not permitted. We cannot add a float64 or even an int32 to an int. It is, nevertheless, allowed to write 1e6*time. Second, or mathematics. 1('t'+2.0) or even Exp(1). Constants, unlike variables, operate like regular numbers in Go.

There are three types of numerical constants: integer, complex, and floating-point.

Integer Constant

- The base or radix is specified by a prefix: 0x or 0X for hexadecimal, 0 for octal, and nothing for decimal.

- An integer literal can additionally include a suffix that is a mix of U(upper case) and L(upper case), indicating that it is unsigned or long.

- It can be a constant in decimal, octal, or hexadecimal form.

- An int can only store a 64-bit integer at most, and occasionally less.

Here are some instances of Integer Constant:

```
85        : decimal
0213      : octal
0x4b      : hexadecimal
30        : int
30u       : unsigned int
30l       : long
30ul      : unsigned long
212       : Legal
215u      : Legal
0xFeeL    : Legal
078       : Illegal: 8 is not an octal digit
032UU     : Illegal: cannot repeat a suffix
```

Complex Constant Complex constants act pretty similarly to floating-point constants. It is an ordered or real pair of integer constant (or parameters), separated by a comma and contained in parentheses. The first constant represents the actual component, while the second represents the imaginary part. COMPLEX*8 is a complex constant that requires 8 bytes of storage.

Example:

```
(0.0, 0.0) (-123.456E+30, 987.654E-29)
```

Floating Constant   An integer portion, a decimal point, a fractional part, and an exponent part comprise a floating type constant.

Floating constants can be represented in either decimal or exponential forms.

When expressing in decimal form, we must include the decimal point, the exponent, or both.

And, when employing the exponential form, the integer, fractional, or both parts must include.

Here are some instances of Floating type constants:

```
3.14159      : Legal
314159E-5L   : Legal
510E         : Illegal: incomplete exponent
210f         : Illegal: no decimal or exponent
.e55         : Illegal: missing integer or fraction
```

String Literals

Go supports two forms of string literals: " " (double-quote style) and ' ' (back-quote).

The + and += operators can use to concatenate strings.

Characters in a string are comparable to character literals in that they are plain characters, escape sequences, and universal characters.

And this is a case of untyped.

String types with zero values are blank strings, which can be represented by " " or " in literal.

String types may all be compared using operators such as ==,!=, and (for comparing of same types)

Syntax:

```
type _string struct
{
```

```
    elements *byte // the underlying bytes
    len   int   //the  number of bytes
}
```

Example:

```
"hello, peeksofpeeks"
"hello, \
peeksofpeeks"
"hello " "peeks" "ofpeeks"
```

All three of the above statements are similar in this context in that they lack a specific type.

Example:

```
package main
import "fmt"
func main()
{
    const X = "POP"
    var Y = "PeeksofPeeks"
    // Concat strings.
    var helloEveryone = X+ " " + Y
    helloEveryone += "!"
    fmt.Println(helloEveryone)

    // Compare strings.
    fmt.Println(X == "POP")
    fmt.Println(Y < X)
}
```

Boolean Constant

String constants and Boolean constants are both types of constants. It follows the same guidelines as a string constant. The main difference is that it contains two untyped constants, true and false.

Example:

```
package main
import "fmt"
const Pi = 3.14
```

```go
func main()
{
    const trueConst = true
    // Type definition using the type keyword
    type myBool bool
    var defaultBool = trueConst // allowed
    var customBool myBool = trueConst // allowed
    //  defaultBool = customBool // not allowed
    fmt.Println(defaultBool)
    fmt.Println(customBool)
}
```

VARIABLE SCOPE IN Go

A variable's scope may be described as the area of the program where a specific variable is available. A variable can declare in a class, method, loop, or other structure. Like C/C++, all identifiers in GoLang are lexically (or statically) scoped, which means that the variable's scope may determine at compilation time. Alternatively, a variable can only be called from within the code block in which it is defined.

Variable scope rules in GoLang may be classified into two types based on where the variables are declared:

- Local Variables (declared inside a block)

- Global Variables (declared outside a block)

Local Variables

- The type of variables that are defined within a function or a block is known as local variables. Outside of the function or block, these are inaccessible.

- These variables can also be declared within a function's for, while, and similar statements.

- These variables, however, can be accessed by nested code blocks within a function.

- The block variables are another name for these variables.

- A compile-time error will occur if these variables are declared twice with the same name in the same scope.

- After the function's execution is complete, these variables are no longer present.

- The variable specified outside the loop is also available within the nested loops. It signifies that a global variable will be available to all methods and loops. The loop and function within the function will access the local variable.

- A variable declared within a loop body is not visible to the outside of the loop body.

Example:

```
// Program to illustrate the local variables
package main
import "fmt"
// main function
func main() { // from here the local level scope
of main function starts
 // local variables inside the main function
 var myvariable1, myvariable2 int = 90, 47
// Display values of the variables
fmt.Printf("Value of myvariable1 is : %d\n",
                                   myvariable1)
fmt.Printf("Value of myvariable2 is : %d\n",
                                   myvariable2)
} // here the local level scope of main function
ends
```

Global Variables

- Global variables are specified outside of a function or a block.

- These are accessible for the duration of a program.

- These are declared outside of any functions or blocks at the program's top.

- These are accessible from anywhere in the program.

Example:

```
// Program to illustrate the global variables
package main
```

```
import "fmt"
// the global variable declaration
var myvariable1 int = 120
func main() { // from here the local level scope
starts
// the local variables inside the main function
var myvariable2 int = 210
// Display value of global variable
fmt.Printf("Value of Global myvariable1 is :
%d\n",
                            myvariable1)
// Display value of local variable
fmt.Printf("Value of Local myvariable2 is : %d\n",
                            myvariable2)
// calling function
display()
} // local level scope ends
// taking function
func display() { // the local level starts
// Display value of global variable
fmt.Printf("Value of Global myvariable1 is :
%d\n",
                            myvariable1)
} // the local scope ends here
```

Note: What happens if a local variable with the same name as a global variable appears within a function? The solution is straightforward: the compiler will favor the local variable. When two similar variables with the same name are declared, the compiler usually generates a compile-time error. However, if the variables are specified in distinct scopes, the compiler will accept them. The compiler will precedence the local variable when a local variable with the same name as a global variable is declared.

- In the following example, we can see the output. As the value of myvariable1 in function main is 210. As a result, a local variable strongly prefers a global variable.

Example:

```
// Program to show the compiler giving preference
// to local variable over a global variable
```

```
package main
import "fmt"
// the global variable declaration
var myvariable1 int = 120
func main() { // from here the local level scope
starts
// local variables inside main function
// it is same as a global variable
var myvariable1 int = 210
// Display value
fmt.Printf("Value of myvariable1 is : %d\n",
                  myvariable1)
} // here the local level scope ends
```

DECLARATION OF MULTIPLE VARIABLES

A single statement can use to declare many variables.

The syntax for multiple variable declaration is var name1, name2 type = initialvalue1, initialvalue2.

Example:

```
package main
import "fmt"
func main() {
    var width, height int = 120, 60 //declaring
multiple variables
    fmt.Println("width :", width, "height :", height)
}
```

If the variables have an initial value, the type can be omitted. Because the variables in the preceding program have initial values, the int type may delete.

Example:

```
package main
import "fmt"
func main() {
    var width, height = 120, 60 //"int" is dropped
    fmt.Println("width :", width, "height :", height)
}
```

As an example, the above software will print width of 120 and a height of 60 as a result.

It's pretty clear you should have guessed by now, if no starting value is specified for width and height, that we will set to 0.

Example:

```
package main
import "fmt"
func main() {
    var width, height int
    fmt.Println("width :", width, "height :", height)
    width = 120
    height = 60
    fmt.Println("new width :", width, "new height
:", height)
}
```

There may be chances when we want to define variables of several kinds in a single sentence. The syntax for doing so is explained below:

```
var (
    nme1 = initialvalue1
    nme2 = initialvalue2
)
```

The following program declares variables of various kinds using the syntax described above.

```
package main
import "fmt"
func main() {
    var (
        name   = "natasha"
        age    = 27
        height int
    )
    fmt.Println("my name :", name, ", age :", age,
"and height :", height)
}
```

Here, we define a string variable name, an int variable age, and an int variable height.

Shorthand Declaration

Go also has a more compact approach to declaring variables. This is referred to as a shorthand statement, and it employs the := operator.

The shorthand form for declaring a variable is name := initialvalue.

The following program declares a variable count with a value of 12 using the shorthand syntax. Because count has been started with the integer value 12, Go will infer that it is of type int.

```
package main
import "fmt"
func main() {
    count := 12
    fmt.Println("Count =",count)
}
```

Multiple variables can also be declared on a single line using shorthand syntax.

```
package main
import "fmt"
func main() {
    name, age := "natasha", 27 //short hand
declaration
    fmt.Println("my name :", name, "age :", age)
}
```

The preceding program defines two variables of type string and int, respectively.

If we execute or run the above program, we will see my name, natasha, and age, 27 printed.

Shorthand declaration necessitates the assignment of initial values to all variables on the left side of the assignment. The following application will output an assignment mismatch error: two variables but only one value. This is because age has not been assigned a value.

```
package main
import "fmt"
func main() {
    name, age := "natasha" //error
    fmt.Println("my name :", name, "age :", age)
}
```

Only when at least one of the variables on the left side of := is newly defined may shorthand syntax be used. Think about the following program:

```
package main
import "fmt"
func main() {
    x, y := 30, 10 // declare variables x and y
    fmt.Println("x is", x, "y is", y)
    y, z := 50, 60 // y is already declared but z is
new
    fmt.Println("y is", y, "z is", z)
    y, z = 70, 80 // assign new values to already
declared variables y and z
    fmt.Println("changed y is", y, "z is", z)
}
```

In contrast, if we execute the following program:

```
package main
import "fmt"
func main() {
    x, y := 20, 30 //x and y declared
    fmt.Println("x is", x, "y is", y)
    x, y := 40, 50 //error, no new variables
}
```

It will output the error message. There are no new variables on the left side of := since variables a and b have already been declared. There are no new variables on the left side of := in line no. 6.

Variables can also have values that are calculated during run time. Think about the following program:

```
package main
import (
    "fmt"
    "math"
)
func main() {
    x, y := 145.8, 543.8
    z := math.Min(x, y)
    fmt.Println("Minimum value :", z)
}
```

Math is a package in the program above, and Min is a function within that package. We need to know that the value of z is determined at run time and equals the sum of x and y.

Variables specified as belonging to one type cannot be assigned a value of another type because Go is tightly typed. Because age is specified as type int, and we are attempting to assign a string value, the following program will show an error stating that we cannot use "natasha" (type string) as type int in the assignment.

```
package main
func main() {
    age := 27       // age is int
    age = "natasha" // error since we are trying to
assign the string to a variable of type int
}
```

This chapter covered how to name a variable, scope, and constants. Moreover, we also discussed defining multiple variables and Shorthand declaration.

CHAPTER 5

Operators and Control Structures

IN THIS CHAPTER

> ➤ For

> ➤ If

> ➤ Switch

> ➤ Operators

In Chapter 4, we covered variables where we discussed how to name a variable and multiple variables. We also covered scope and constants. This chapter will discuss control statements with for, if, and switch. Moreover, we will cover operators with their relevant examples.

OPERATORS IN Go

Operators are the building blocks of every programming language. As a result, without the usage of operators, the functionality of the Go language is incomplete. Operators allow us to do numerous actions on operands. Operators in the Go programming language are classified based on their functionality:

- Arithmetic Operators

- Relational Operators

DOI: 10.1201/9781003310457-5   **57**

- Misc Operators

- Bitwise Operators

- Assignment Operators

- Logical Operators

Arithmetic Operators

In Go, these are used to execute arithmetic/mathematical operations on operands:

- **Addition:** The '+' operator joins two operands together. For instance, x+y.

- **Subtraction:** The '−' operator takes two operands and subtracts them. For example, x-y.

- **Multiplication:** The '*' is used to multiply the two operands. For instance, x*y.

- **Division:** The '/' operator divides first operand by second operand. As an example, consider x/y.

- **Modulus:** When first operand is divided by the second, the remainder of the '%' operator returns. For instance, x percent y.

Nota bene: -, +, !, &, *, and - are also known as unary operators, and their precedence is higher. Because ++ and -- operators originate from statements rather than expressions; they are outside the operator hierarchy.

Example:

```
// Program to illustrate the
// use of the arithmetic operators
package main
import "fmt"
func main()
{
    x:= 37
    y:= 22
    // Addition
    result1:= x + y
    fmt.Printf("Result of x + y = %d", result1)
```

```
    // Subtraction
    result2 := x - y
    fmt.Printf("\nResult of x - y = %d", result2)
    // Multiplication
    result3 := x * y
    fmt.Printf("\nResult of x * y = %d", result3)
    // Division
    result4 := x / y
    fmt.Printf("\nResult of x / y = %d", result4)
    // Modulus
    result5 := x % y
    fmt.Printf("\nResult of x %% y = %d", result5)
}
```

Relational Operators

When comparing two values, relational operators are employed. Let's have a look at them:

- The '==' (Equal To) operator determines whether or not the two operands are equal. If this is the case, it returns the true. If not, it returns false. 6==6 will, for example, return true.

- The '!=' operator determines whether the two provided operands are equal or not. If it does, it returns true. If it does not, it returns false. It is the boolean equivalent of the '==' operator. 6!=6 will, for example, return false.

- The '>' (Greater Than) operator determines if the first operand is greater than the second. If this is the case, it returns the true. If not, it returns false. 7>6 will, for example, yield true.

- The '<' (Less Than) operator determines if the first operand is less than the second. If this is the case, it returns the true. If not, it returns false. 6<4, for example, will return false.

- The '≥' (Greater Than Equal To) operator determines if the first operand is greater than or equal to the second operand then it returns true. If not, it returns false. 6≥6 will, for example, return true.

- The '≤' (Least Than Equal To) operator determines if the first operand is less than or equal to the second operand then it returns true. If not, it returns false. 6≤6 will, for example, also return true.

Example:

```go
// Program to illustrate
// the use of relational operators
package main
import "fmt"
func main() {
    x:= 38
    y:= 25
    // '==' (Equal To)
    result1:= x == y
    fmt.Println(result1)
    // '!=' (Not Equal To)
    result2:= x != y
    fmt.Println(result2)
    // '<' (Less Than)
    result3:= x < y
    fmt.Println(result3)
    // '>' (Greater Than)
    result4:= x > y
    fmt.Println(result4)
    // '>=' (Greater Than Equal To)
    result5:= x >= y
    fmt.Println(result5)
    // '<=' (Less Than Equal To)
    result6:= x <= y
    fmt.Println(result6)
}
```

Logical Operators

They are used to integrate two or more conditions/constraints or complement the original condition's evaluation.

- **Logical AND:** The && operator returns the true when both of the conditions in consideration are met. If not, it returns false. x && y, for example, returns true when both x and y are true (i.e., non-zero).

- **Logical OR:** When one or both of the requirements is met, the '||' operator returns true. If not, it returns false. For instance, x || y returns true if either x or y is true (i.e., non-zero). Naturally, it returns true if both x and y are true.

- **Logical NOT:** If condition in question is satisfied, the '!' operator returns true. If not, it returns false. !x, for example, returns true if a is false, that is, when x=0.

Example:

```
// Program to illustrate
//the use of logical operators
package main
import "fmt"
func main() {
    var x int = 26
    var y int = 65
    if(x!=y && x<=y){
        fmt.Println("True")
    }
    if(x!=y || x<=y){
        fmt.Println("True")
    }
    if(!(x==y)){
        fmt.Println("True")
    }
}
```

Bitwise Operators

In the Go programming language, 6 bitwise operators act at the bit level or conduct bit-by-bit operations. The bitwise operators are:

- **& (bitwise AND):** Takes two operands and performs the AND on each bit of the two numbers. AND returns 1 only if the both bits are 1.

- **| (bitwise OR):** Takes two operands and performs the OR on each bit of the two integers. OR returns value of 1 if either of the two bits is 1.

- **^ (bitwise XOR):** Takes two operands and performs the XOR on each bit of the two numbers. If two bits are different, the result of XOR is 1.

- **<< (left shift):** Takes two integers, left shifts the bits of the first operand, and the second operand specifies the number of positions to shift.

- **>> (right shift):** Takes two numbers, shifts the first operand's bits to the right, and number of places to shift is determined by the second operand.

- **&^ (AND NOT):** This is a straightforward operator.

Example:

```
// Program to illustrate
// the use of bitwise operators
package main
import "fmt"
func main() {
   x:= 34
   y:= 20
   // & (bitwise AND)
   result1:= x & y
   fmt.Printf("Result of x & y = %d", result1)
   // | (bitwise OR)
   result2:= x | y
   fmt.Printf("\nResult of p | q = %d", result2)
   // ^ (bitwise XOR)
   result3:= p ^ q
   fmt.Printf("\nResult of x ^ y = %d", result3)
   // << (left shift)
   result4:= x << 1
   fmt.Printf("\nResult of x << 1 = %d", result4)
   // >> (right shift)
   result5:= x >> 1
   fmt.Printf("\nResult of x >> 1 = %d", result5)
   // &^ (AND NOT)
   result6:= x &^ y
   fmt.Printf("\nResult of x &^ y = %d", result6)
}
```

Assignment Operators

When assigning a value to a variable, assignment operators are employed. The assignment operator's left operand is a variable, while the assignment operator's right operand is a value. The value on the right side must have the same data type as the variable on the left side, or the compiler will throw an error. The following are examples of assignment operators:

- **"=" (Simple Assignment):** The most basic assignment operator. The value on the right is assigned to the variable on the left using this operator.

- **"+=" (Add Assignment):** A combination of the '+' and '=' operators. This operator first adds the variable on the left's current value to the right and then assigns result to the variable on the left.

- **"-=" (Subtract Assignment):** A combination of the '−' and '=' operators. This operator subtracts the variable on the left's current value from the right and then assigns the result to the variable on the left.

- **"*=" (Multiply Assignment):** A combination of the '*' and '=' operators. This operator first multiplies the variable on the left to the right and then assigns the result to the left variable.

- **"/=" (Division Assignment):** A combination of the '/' and '=' operators. This operator divides the variable on the left's current value by the value on the right and then assigns result to the variable on the left.

- **"%=" (Modulus Assignment):** This operator combines the '%' and '=' operators. This operator multiplies current value of the variable on the left to the right and then assigns the result to the left variable.

- **"&=" (Bitwise AND Assignment):** A combination of the '&' and '=' operators. This operator "Bitwise AND" the current value to the left variable to the right before assigning the result to the left variable.

- **"=" (Bitwise Exclusive OR):** A combination of the "=" and '=' operators. This operator "Bitwise Exclusive OR" the current value of the left variable to the right before assigning the result to the left variable.

- **"|=" (Bitwise Inclusive OR):** A combination of the '|' and '=' operators. This operator "Bitwise Inclusive OR" the current value of the left variable to the right before assigning the result to the left variable.

Example:

```go
// Program to illustrate
// the use of assignment operators
package main
import "fmt"
func main()
{
    var x int = 49
     var y int = 54
    // "="(Simple Assignment)
    x = y
    fmt.Println(p)
    // "+="(Add Assignment)
     x += y
    fmt.Println(x)
    //"-="(Subtract Assignment)
    x-=y
    fmt.Println(x)
    // "*="(Multiply Assignment)
    x*= y
    fmt.Println(x)
    // "/="(Division Assignment)
     x /= y
    fmt.Println(x)
     // "%="(Modulus Assignment)
     x %= y
    fmt.Println(x)
}
```

Misc Operators

- **&:** This operator returns the variable's address.

- ***:** This operator returns a pointer to a variable.

- **<-:** This operator's name is received. It's used to get a value from the channel.

Example:

```go
// Program to illustrate
// the use of Misc Operators
```

```go
package main
import "fmt"
func main() {
    x := 6
    // Using address of operator(&) and
    // pointer indirection(*) operator
    y := &x
    fmt.Println(*y)
    *y = 7
    fmt.Println(x)
}
```

CONTROL STATEMENTS

The programmer must define one or more conditions to be evaluated or tested by the program, a statement or statements to be performed if the condition is determined to be true, and optionally, further statements to be run if the condition is decided to be false.

The general form of a common decision-making framework present in most programming languages is shown below.

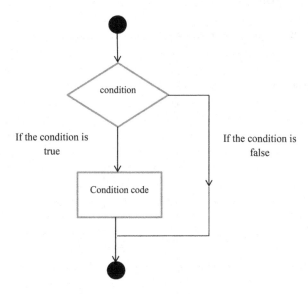

Structure of decision making.

The Go programming language supports the following decision-making statements.

Sr. No	Statement and Description
1	if statement A Boolean expression is followed by one or more statements in an if statement.
2	if...else statement When Boolean expression is false, the if an optional else statement follows statement.
3	nested if statements The if or else if statement can be used inside another if or else if statement(s).
4	switch statement A switch statement checks a variable for equality against a set of values.
5	select statement A select statement is similar to a switch statement; however, case statements relate to channel communications.

if Statement

This is the most straightforward decision-making statement. It is used to decide whether or not a specific statement or block of statements will be performed, i.e., if a given condition is true, then a block of statements is executed, otherwise not.

Syntax:

```
if(condition)
{
    // Statement to execute if condition is true
}
```

Flowchart:

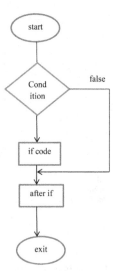

Statement of if.

Example:

```go
// Program to illustrate
//the use of if statement
package main
import "fmt"
func main() {
    // taking local variable
    var v int = 800
    // using the if statement for
    // checking condition
    if(v < 2000) {
        // print following if
        // condition evaluates to true
        fmt.Printf("v is less than 2000\n")
    }
    fmt.Printf("Value of v is : %d\n", v)
}
```

if...else Statement

The if statement by itself informs us that the condition is true, a block of statements will be executed; if condition is false, the block of statements will not be executed. But what if the condition is false and we want to do something else? This is when the otherwise statement comes in. When the condition is false, we may use the else statement in combination with the if statement to run a code block.

Syntax:

```go
 if (condition)
{
    // Executes this block if
    // the condition is true
} else {
    // Executes this block if
    // the condition is false
}
```

Flowchart:

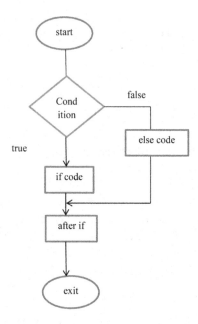

Statement of if-else.

Example:

```
// Program to illustrate
// the use of if...else statement
package main
import "fmt"
func main() {
    // taking a local variable
    var v int = 2400
    // using the if statement for
    // checking condition
    if(v < 2000) {
        // print following if
        // the condition evaluates to true
        fmt.Printf("v is less than 2000\n")
    } else {
        // print following if
        // the condition evaluates to true
        fmt.Printf("v is greater than 2000\n")
    }
}
```

Nested if Statement

In Go, a nested if is an if statement that is the target of another if or else expression. An if statement nested inside another if statement is referred to as a nested if statement. Yes, we may nest if statements within if statements in GoLang. In other words, we may nest an if statement within another if statement.

Syntax:

```
if (condition1) {
    // Executes when the condition1 is true
    if (condition2) {
        // Executes when the condition2 is true
    }
}
```

Flowchart:

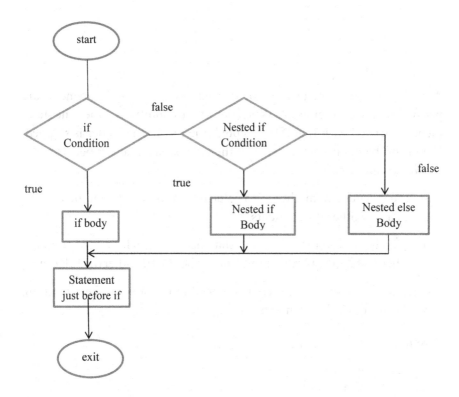

Statement of nested-if.

Example:

```
// Program to illustrate
// the use of nested if statement
package main
import "fmt"
func main() {
    // taking the two local variable
    var v1 int = 500
    var v2 int = 800
    // using if statement
    if( v1 == 600 ) {
        // if condition is true then
        // check the following
        if( v2 == 800 )  {
            // if the condition is true
            // then display following
            fmt.Printf("Value of v1 is 500 and v2 is
800\n" );
        }
    }
}
```

if..else..if Ladder

A user can select from a variety of alternatives here. The if statements are performed in the order listed. When one of the conditions is met, the statement associated with that if is executed; the rest of the ladder is skipped. If none of the requirements are met, the last else statement is performed.

Important Notes:

• The if statement might have a value of zero or one, and it must occur after any other if statements.

• The else if statement in an if statement can include zero to many other if statements, and it must occur before the otherwise clause.

• If an else if succeeds, there is no need to try none of the remaining else if's or else's statements.

Syntax:

```
if(condition_1) {
        // this block will execute when the
condition_1 is true
```

```
} else if(condition_2) {
    // this block will execute when the condition2
is true
}
....
else {
      // this block will execute when none
      // of condition is true
}
```

Flowchart:

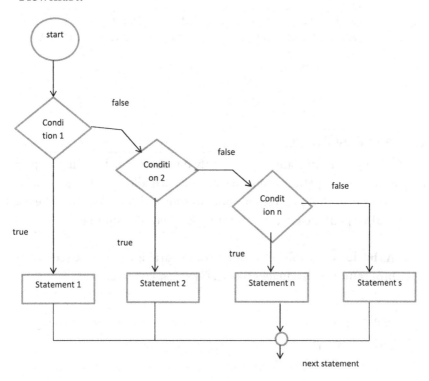

Statement of if-else-if.

Example:

```
// Program to illustrate
// the use of if..else..if ladder
package main
import "fmt"
func main() {
```

```
        // taking a local variable
    var v1 int = 800
      // checking condition
    if(v1 == 120) {
        // if condition is true then
        // display following */
        fmt.Printf("Value of v1 is 120\n")
    } else if(v1 == 250) {
        fmt.Printf("Value of a is 250\n")
    } else if(v1 == 310) {
        fmt.Printf("Value of a is 310\n")
    } else {
        // if none of the conditions is true
        fmt.Printf("None of values is matching\n")
    }
}
```

Go LANGUAGE LOOPS

The Go programming language has only one loop, which is a for loop. For loop is a form of repetition control structure that allows us to design a loop that will be executed a certain number of times. This for loop may be used in several ways in the Go programming language, including:

1. **As basic as possible for loop:** It is comparable to what we see in other programming languages like C, C++, C#, Java, etc.

   Syntax:

   ```
   for initialization; condition; post{
           // statement
   }
   ```

   Here, the initialization statement is optional and runs before the for loop begins. The initialization statement is always contained within a basic statement, such as variable declarations, increment or assignment instructions, or function calls.

   The condition statement contains a Boolean expression evaluated at the start of each loop iteration. The loop is executed if the conditional statement's value is true.

The post statement is performed after the for loop body. Following the post statement, the condition statement is re-evaluated; if the value of the conditional statement is false, the loop is terminated.

Example:

```
/ Program to illustrate
// the use of simple for loop
package main
import "fmt"
// the main function
func main() {
    // for loop
    // This loop starts when x = 0
    // executes till x<4 condition is true
    // post statement is x++
    for x := 0; x < 4; x++{
      fmt.Printf("helloeveryone\n")
      }
}
```

2. **For loop as infinite loop:** By deleting all three expressions from the for loop, a for loop may be utilized as an infinite loop. When a user does not include a condition statement in a for loop, it indicates that the condition statement is true, and loop enters an endless loop.

Syntax:

```
for
{
    // Statement(s)
}
```

Example:

```
// Program to illustrate
// the use of an infinite loop
package main
  import "fmt"
// the main function
```

```
func main() {
    // infinite loop
    for {
       fmt.Printf("Helloeveryone\n")
    }
}
```

3. **while for loop:** A for loop can also be used as a while loop. This loop is repeated until the specified condition is met. The loop is terminated when the value of the provided condition is false.

Syntax:

```
for condition{
    // statements
}
```

Example:

```
/ Program to illustrate
// for loop as while Loop
package main
import "fmt"
// the main function
func main() {
    // while loop for loop executes till
    // x < 3 condition is true
    x:= 0
    for x < 3 {
        x += 2
    }
    fmt.Println(x)
}
```

4. **Simple range in for loop:** The range may also be used for a loop.

Syntax:

```
for x, y:= range rvariable{
    // statements
}
```

Here, the variables x and y are where the iteration values are stored. They are sometimes referred to as iteration variables.

The second variable, y, is not required.

Before the loop begins, the range expression is evaluated once.

Example:

```go
// Program to illustrate
// the use of simple range loop
package main
import "fmt"
// the main function
func main() {
    // Here rvariable is array
    rvariable:= []string{"HEW", "Hello",
"Helloeveryoneworld"}
    // x and y stores the value of rvariable
    // x store index number of individual string
and
    // y store individual string of the given
array
    for x, y:= range rvariable {
        fmt.Println(x, y)
    }
}
```

5. **Using a for loop for strings:** A for loop can iterate across a string's Unicode code point.

Syntax:

```go
for index, chr:= range str{
    // Statements
}
```

Here, the index is a variable that stores the first byte of a UTF-8 encoded code point, chr is a variable that stores the characters of the provided string, and str is a string.

Example:

```go
// Program to illustrate
// the use for loop using string
```

```
package main
import "fmt"
// the main function
func main() {
    // String as range in the for loop
    for x, y:= range "XxyCd" {
        fmt.Printf("Index number of %U is %d\n",
y, x)
    }
}
```

6. **For maps:** A for loop can traverse across the map's key and value pairs.

Syntax:

```
for key, value := range map {
    // Statements
}
```

Example:

```
// Program to illustrate
// the use for loop using maps
package main
import "fmt"
// the main function
func main() {
    // using the maps
    mmap := map[int]string{
        22:"Peeks",
        33:"POP",
        44:"PeeksofPeeks",
    }
    for key, value:= range mmap {
        fmt.Println(key, value)
    }
}
```

7. **For channel:** A for loop can iterate over the consecutive data transmitted on the channel until the channel is closed.

Syntax:

```
for item := range Chnl {
    // statement(s)
}
```

Example:

```
// program to illustrate
// the use for loop using channel
package main
import "fmt"
// the main function
func main() {
    // using the channel
    chnl := make(chan int)
    go func(){
        chnl <- 1000
        chnl <- 10000
        chnl <- 100000
        chnl <- 1000000
        close(chnl)
    }()
    for x:= range chnl {
        fmt.Println(x)
    }
}
```

Important Notes:

- Parentheses do not enclose a for loop's three statements.

- Curly braces are required for the loop.

- The opening brace and the post statement should be on the same line.

- If array, string, slice, or map is empty, the for loop does not throw an error and proceeds with its flow. In other words, if array, string, slice, or map is nil, the number of for loop iterations is zero.

Go SWITCH STATEMENT

A switch statement is an example of a multiway branch statement. It offers an effective method for transferring execution to various code areas according to the expression's value. The Go programming language allows two types of switch statements:

- Expression Switch
- Type Switch

Expression Switch

The expression switch is analogous to the switch statement in C, C++, and Java. It allows us to efficiently route execution to various areas of code based on the value of the expression.

Syntax:

```
switch optstatement; optexpression{
case expression1: Statement
case expression2: Statement
.
.
default: Statement
}
```

Important Notes:

- In the expression switch, both optstatement and optexpression are optional statements.

- If both optstatement and optexpression are present, a semi-colon (;) must be used to separate them.

- If there is no expression in the switch, the compiler assumes that the expression is true.

- The optional statement, often known as the optstatement, comprises basic statements like variable declarations, increment or assignment statements, function calls, etc.

- If a variable appears in the optional statement, its scope is confined to that switch statement.

- There is no break statement in switch statement's case and default statements. However, we may utilize the break and fallthrough statements if our application requires them.

- In a switch statement, the default statement is optional.

- A case can have multiple values separated by a comma (,).

- If a case lacks an expression, the compiler assumes that the expression is true.

First example:

```
// Program to illustrate
// the concept of Expression switch statement
package main
import "fmt"
func main() {
    // the switch statement with both
    // optional statement, i.e, day:=4
    // and the expression, i.e, day
    switch day:=5; day{
        case 1:
        fmt.Println("Sunday")
        case 2:
        fmt.Println("Monday")
        case 3:
        fmt.Println("Tuesday")
        case 4:
        fmt.Println("Wednesday")
        case 5:
        fmt.Println("Thursday")
        case 6:
        fmt.Println("Friday")
        case 7:
        fmt.Println("Saturday")
        default:
        fmt.Println("Invalid")
    }
}
```

Second example:

```
// Program to illustrate
// the concept of Expression switch statement
package main
import "fmt"
```

```go
func main() {
    var value int = 3
    // Switch statement without an
    // optional statement and expression
    switch {
        case value == 1:
        fmt.Println("Hey")
        case value == 2:
        fmt.Println("Hello")
        case value == 3:
        fmt.Println("Namstae")
        default:
        fmt.Println("Invalid")
    }
}
```

Third example:

```go
// Program to illustrate
// the concept of Expression switch statement
package main
import "fmt"
func main() {
    var value string = "four"
    // Switch statement without the default
statement
    // Multiple values in the case statement
    switch value {
        case "one":
        fmt.Println("C")
        case "two", "three":
        fmt.Println("C#")
        case "four", "five", "six":
        fmt.Println("Go")
    }
}
```

Type Switch

When comparing types, a type switch is applied. The case in this switch includes the type that will compare to the type in the switch expression.

Syntax:

```
switch optstatement; typeswitchexpression{
case typelist 1: Statement
case typelist 2: Statement
.
.
default: Statement
}
```

Important Notes:

- The optional statement, abbreviated as optstatement, is comparable to the switch expression.

- A case can have multiple values separated by a comma (,).

- The case and default statements in the type switch statement do not contain break statements. However, we may utilize the break and fallthrough statements if our application requires them.

- In a type switch statement, the default statement is optional.

- The typeswitchexpression is an expression that produces a type as a consequence.

- If an expression is assigned to a variable in typeswitchexpression using the := operator, the type of that variable is determined by the type contained in the case clause. If the case clause includes two or more types, the variable's type is the type in which it is generated in typeswitchexpression.

Example:

```
// Program to illustrate
// the concept of Type switch statement
package main
import "fmt"
func main() {
    var value interface{}
    switch x:= value.(type) {
        case bool:
        fmt.Println("The value is of boolean type")
        case float64:
```

```
        fmt.Println("The value is of float64 type")
        case int:
        fmt.Println("value is of int type")
        default:
        fmt.Printf("value is of type: %T", x)
    }
}
```

This chapter covered control structures where we discussed switch statements, if-else, and nested if. Moreover, we also covered loops and operators with their relevant syntax and examples.

CHAPTER 6

Arrays, Slices, and Maps

IN THIS CHAPTER

➢ Arrays

➢ Slices

➢ Strings

➢ Maps

Chapter 5 covered switch statements, operators, if-else, and nested if. We also covered the loop with its relevant syntax and examples. In this chapter, we will discuss arrays, slices, and maps.

ARRAYS

Arrays in the GoLang computer language are similar to those in other programming languages. In the software, we may need to keep a collection of data of the same type, such as a list of students' marks. An Array is used to hold this sort of collection in a program. An array is a fixed-length sequence utilized in memory to hold homogenous items. Because of their limited length array is not as popular as Slice in the Go language.

An array can have zero or more than zero elements stored in it. The array elements are indexed using the [] index operator with their zero-based position, which means that the index of first element is array[0], and the index of the final element is array[len(array)-1].

Creating and Accessing an Array

Arrays are formed in two methods in the Go programming language.

DOI: 10.1201/9781003310457-6

Using the var Keyword

In Go, an array of a specific type with a name, size, and items is created using the var keyword.

Syntax:

```
Var arrayname[length]Type
```

or

```
var arrayname[length]Typle{item1, item2, item3,
...itemN}
```

Important Notes:

- Arrays in Go are mutable; therefore, we may apply array[index] syntax on the left-hand side of the assignment to set the array's elements to the provided index.

```
Var arrayname[index] = element
```

- We may access the array's elements using the index value or a for a loop.

- The array type in the Go programming language is one-dimensional.

- The array's length is fixed and cannot be changed.

- Duplicate elements may be stored in an array.

Example:

```
// Program to illustrate how to
// create an array using var keyword
// and accessing elements of
// the array using their index value
package main
import "fmt"
func main() {
// Creating array of string type
// Using the var keyword
var myarr[3]string
```

```
// Elements are assigned using the index
myarr[0] = "HEW"
myarr[1] = "Helloevryoneoworld"
myarr[2] = "Hello"
// Accessing elements of the array
// Using the index value
fmt.Println("Elements of Array:")
fmt.Println("Element 1: ", myarr[0])
fmt.Println("Element 2: ", myarr[1])
fmt.Println("Element 3: ", myarr[2])
}
```

Using a Shorthand Declaration

Arrays in Go may also be declared using a shorthand declaration. It is more flexible than the initial assertion.

Syntax:

```
arrayname:= [length]Type{item1, item2, item3,...
itemN}
```

Example:

```
// Program to illustrate how to create
// array using shorthand declaration
// and accessing elements of
// the array using for loop
package main
import "fmt"
func main() {
// Shorthand declaration of the array
arr:= [4]string{"hello", "hew", "Hello1431",
"Helloeveryoneworld"}
// Accessing elements of the
// array Using for loop
fmt.Println("Elements of the array:")
for x:= 0; x < 3; x++{
fmt.Println(arr[x])
}
}
```

Multidimensional Array

Although we already know that arrays are one-dimensional, we can create a multidimensional array. Arrays of the same kind are known as multidimensional arrays. We may build a multidimensional array in Go by using the following syntax:

```
Arrayname [Length1] [Length2] .. [LengthN] Type
```

As demonstrated in the example below, we may build a multidimensional array using the Var keyword or a shorthand declaration.

Note: If a cell is not initialized with a value by the user in a multidimension array, the compiler will do so automatically. There is no such thing as uninitialized concept in GoLang.

Example:

```
// Program to illustrate
// the concept of multi-dimension array
package main
import "fmt"
func main() {
// Creating, initializing
// 2-dimensional array
// Using the shorthand declaration
// Here (,) Comma is necessary
arry:= [3] [3] string{{"C", "C++", "PHP"},
                      {"Go", "C#", "Scala"},
                      {"Python", "C#", "HTML"},}
// Accessing values of
// the array Using for loop
fmt.Println("Elements of Array 1")
for a:= 0; a < 3; a++{
for b:= 0; b < 3; b++{
fmt.Println(arry[a] [b])
}
}
// Creating a 2-dimensional
// array using the var keyword
// and initializing a multi
// -dimensional array using index
var arry1 [2] [2] int
```

```
arry1[0][0] = 100
arry1[0][1] = 200
arry1[1][0] = 300
arry1[1][1] = 400
// Accessing values of the array
fmt.Println("Elements of the array 2")
for x:= 0; x<2; x++{
for y:= 0; y<2; y++{
fmt.Println(arry1[x][y])
}
}
}
```

Important Observations about the Array

1. If an array is not explicitly initialized, the default value of this array is 0.

   Example:

   ```
   // Program to illustrate an array
   package main
   import "fmt"
   func main() {
   // Creating an array of the int type
   // which stores the two elements
   // Here, we do not initialize
   // array so the value of array
   // is zero
   var myarry[2]int
   fmt.Println("Elements of the Array :", myarry)
   }
   ```

2. The length of an array may be find using the len() function, as seen in the following example:

   ```
   // Program to illustrate how to find
   // length of the array
   package main
   import "fmt"
   func main() {
   ```

```
// Creating array
// Using the shorthand declaration
arry1:= [3]int{9,7,6}
arry2:= [...]int{9,7,6,4,5,3,2,4}
arry3:= [3]int{9,3,5}
// Finding length of the
// array using the len method
fmt.Println("The Length of the array 1 is:",
len(arry1))
fmt.Println("The Length of the array 2 is:",
len(arry2))
fmt.Println("The Length of the array 3 is:",
len(arry3))
}
```

3. If the ellipsis "…" appears at the place of length in an array, the array's length is determined by the initialized items. As illustrated in the following example:

```
// Program to illustrate
// the concept of ellipsis in an array
package main
import "fmt"
func main() {
// Creating an array whose size is determined
// by number of elements present in it
// Using the ellipsis
myarray:= [...]string{"HEW", "hew", "hello",
                "Helloeveryoneworld", "HELLO"}
fmt.Println("Elements of array: ", myarray)
// Length of array
// is determine by
// Using the len() method
fmt.Println("Length of array is:", len(myarray))
}
```

4. We can iterate over the array's elements by iterating over the array's range. As illustrated in the following example:

```
// Program to illustrate
// how to iterate array
package main
```

```
import "fmt"
func main() {
// Creating an array whose size
// is represented by ellipsis
myarray:= [...]int{79, 49, 29, 20,
                     49, 49, 48, 39}
// Iterate array using for the loop
for y:=0; y < len(myarray); y++{
fmt.Printf("%d\n", myarray[y])
}
}
```

5. An array in Go is of the value type, not the reference type. As a result, when the array is assigned to a new variable, any modifications performed in the new variable have no effect on the original array. As illustrated in the following example:

```
// Program to illustrate value type array
package main
import "fmt"
func main() {
// Creating array whose size
// is represented by ellipsis
my_array:= [...]int{200, 300, 500, 100, 800}
fmt.Println("Original array(Before):", my_array)
// Creating new variable
// and initialize with the my_array
new_array := my_array
fmt.Println("New array(before):", new_array)
// Change value at index 0 to 500
new_array[0] = 500
fmt.Println("The New array(After):", new_array)
fmt.Println("The Original array(After):", my_array)
}
```

6. If the array's element type is equivalent, then the array type is also comparable. As a result, we may directly compare two arrays using the == operator. As illustrated in the following example:

```
// Program to illustrate
// how to compare the two arrays
```

```
package main
import "fmt"
func main() {
// Arrays
arry1:= [3]int{8,7,5}
arry2:= [...]int{8,7,5}
arry3:= [3]int{8,5,3}
// Comparing arrays using == operator
fmt.Println(arry1==arry2)
fmt.Println(arry2==arry3)
fmt.Println(arry1==arry3)
// This will give error because
// type of arr1 and arr4 is mismatch
/*
arry4:= [4]int{8,7,5}
fmt.Println(arry1==arry4)
*/
}
```

In GoLang, How Do We Copy an Array into Another Array?

Arrays in the GoLang computer language are similar to those in other programming languages. In the program, we may need to keep a collection of data of the same type, such as a list of student marks. An Array is used to hold this sort of collection in a program. An array is a fixed-length sequence utilized in memory to hold homogenous items. GoLang does not provide a built-in method for copying one array into another. However, we may make a clone of an array by simply assigning an array by value or reference to a new variable.

If we make a copy of an array by value and modify the original array's values, it will not reflect changes in the copy of that array. And if we make a copy of an array by reference and modify the original array's values, it will reflect the changes in the duplicate of that array. As seen in the following samples:

Syntax:

```
// creating copy of an array by value
arry := arr1
// Creating copy of an array by reference
arry := &arr1
```

Let's look at few instances to assist us understand this concept:

First example:

```go
// Program to illustrate how
// to copy array by value
package main
import "fmt"
func main() {
    // Creating, initializing an array
    // Using the shorthand declaration
    my_arry1 := [5]string{"C", "Go", "Java",
" Scala ", "C#"}

    // Copying array into new variable
    // Here, elements are passed by value
    my_arry2 := my_arry1
    fmt.Println("Array_1: ", my_arry1)
    fmt.Println("Array_2:", my_arry2)
    my_arry1[0] = "C++"
    // when we copy an array
    // into the another array by value
 then changes made in the original
    // array do not reflect in copy of that array
    fmt.Println("\nThe Array_1: ", my_arry1)
    fmt.Println("The Array_2: ", my_arry2)
}
```

Second example:

```go
// Program to illustrate how to
// copy array by reference
package main
import "fmt"
func main() {
    // Creating, initializing an array
    // Using the shorthand declaration
    my_arry1 := [6]int{14, 416, 47, 69, 44, 32}
    // Copying array into new variable
    // Here, elements are passed by reference
    my_arry2 := &my_arry1
    fmt.Println("Array_1: ", my_arry1)
```

```
        fmt.Println("Array_2:", *my_arry2)
        my_arry1[5] = 200000
        // when we copy an array
        // into the another array by reference
        // then changes made in original
        // array will reflect in
        // the copy of that array
        fmt.Println("\nArray_1: ", my_arry1)
        fmt.Println("Array_2:", *my_arry2)
}
```

In GoLang, How Can We Pass an Array to a Function?

Arrays in the GoLang computer language are similar to those in other programming languages. In the program, we may need to keep a collection of data of the same type, such as a list of student grades. An Array is used to hold this sort of collection in a program. An array is a fixed-length sequence utilized in memory to hold homogenous items.

We can send an array as an argument to a function in the Go programming language. To pass an array as an argument to a function, first create a formal parameter with the following syntax:

Syntax:

```
// For the sized array
func function_name(variablename [size]type){
// Code
}
```

We can pass one or more dimensional arrays to the function using this syntax. Let us illustrate this notion with an example:

```
// Program to illustrate how to pass an
// array as an argument in function
package main
 import "fmt"
// This function accept
// an array as argument
func myfun(a [5]int, size int) int {
    var x, val, y int
    for x = 0; x < size; x++ {
        val += a[x]
```

```
    }
    y = val / size
    return y
}
// the main function
func main() {
    // Creating, initializing an array
    var arr = [5]int{57, 29, 69, 25, 14}
    var rest int
    // Passing an array as an argument
    rest = myfun(arr, 5)
    fmt.Printf("Final result is: %d ", rest)
}
```

Explanation: In the example, we have a method called myfun() that takes an array as an input. In main function, we passed arr[5] of int type to the function with the array's size, and the function returned the array's average.

SLICES

Slice is a Go data structure that is more powerful, adaptable, and convenient than an array. Multiple components cannot be placed in the same slice since it is a variable-length sequence comprising elements of the same sort. It's comparable to an array in that it contains a length and an index value. However, the size of the slice may be expanded, unlike an array. Internally, a slice and an array are linked; a slice is a reference to an underlying array. Duplicate elements may be stored in the slice. In a slice, the initial index point is always 0, and the last is (length of slice – 1).

Slice Declaration

A slice is stated similarly to an array, but it does not provide the slice's size. Hence, it may expand and contract as needed.

Syntax:

```
[]T
```

or

```
[]T{}
```

or

```
[]T{value1, value2, value3, ...value n}
```

T denotes the element type in this case. As an example:

```
var myslice[]int
```

Slice Components

A slice is made up of three parts:

- **Pointer:** The pointer is used to point to the first array element available via the slice. It is not required that the indicated element be the first element of the array in this case.

- **Length:** The length of an array is the total number of elements in the array.

- **Capacity:** The greatest size to which it may expand is represented by the capacity.

Let's have a look at each of these components with the aid of an example:

```
// Program to illustrate the
// working of the slice components
package main
import "fmt"
func main() {
    // Array Creation
    arry := [7]string{"This", "is", "the", "example",
                      "of", "Go", "Programming"}
    // Display array
    fmt.Println("Array:", arry)
    // Creating a slice
    myslice := arry[1:6]
    // Display the slice
    fmt.Println("Slice:", myslice)
    // Display the length of slice
    fmt.Printf("The Length of the slice: %d",
len(myslice))
    // Display the capacity of the slice
```

```
    fmt.Printf("\nThe Capacity of the slice: %d",
cap(myslice))
}
```

Explanation: In the preceding example, we generate a slice from an array. Because the slice's lower bound is set to one, the slice's pointer pointed to index 1 here. Therefore, it began accessing items from index 1. The length of the slice is 5, indicating that there are a total of 5 elements in the slice, and the capacity of the slice is 6, indicating that it can store a maximum of 6 items.

How Can We Create and Initialize a Slice?

A slice in Go may be built and started in the following ways:

Using the Slice Literal

Use the slice literal to generate a slice. The construction of a slice literal is similar to that of an array literal, with the exception that you are not permitted to define the size of the slice in the square brackets[]. The slice literal is presented on the right-hand side of this expression in the following example:

```
var myslice1 = []string{"Hello", "from", "Everyone"}
```

Note: Remember that when we create a slice with a string literal, it first creates an array and then returns a slice reference to it.

Example:

```
// Program to illustrate how
// to create a slice using slice literal
package main
import "fmt"
func main() {
    // Creating slice using the var keyword
    var myslice1 = []string{"Hello", "from",
"Everyone"}
    fmt.Println("My Slice 1:", myslice1)
    // Creating a slice
    //using the shorthand declaration
    myslice2 := []int{14, 35, 57, 49, 41, 24, 45}
    fmt.Println("My Slice 2:", myslice2)
}
```

Using an Array

Because the slice is the array's reference, we may build a slice from the provided array. To create a slice from the given array, first specify the lower and upper bound, which implies the slice can accept elements from the array, beginning with the lower bound and ending with the upper bound. It excludes the items from the upper bound above. As illustrated in the following example:

Syntax:

```
arrayname[low:high]
```

This syntax will return a new slice.

Note that the lower bound is 0 by default, while the upper bound is set to the total number of elements in the specified array.

Example:

```
// Program to illustrate how to
// create the slices from array
package main
import "fmt"
func main() {
    // Array Creation
    arry := [4]string{"Hello", "from",
"Developer", "HFD"}
    // Creating slices from given array
    var myslice1 = aryr[1:2]
    myslice2 := arry[0:]
    myslice3 := arry[:2]
    myslice4 := arry[:]
    // Display the result
    fmt.Println("My Array: ", arry)
    fmt.Println("My Slice 1: ", myslice1)
    fmt.Println("My Slice 2: ", myslice2)
    fmt.Println("My Slice 3: ", myslice3)
    fmt.Println("My Slice 4: ", myslice4)
}
```

Using an Existing Slice

It is possible to create a new slice from the supplied slice. To create a new slice from the given slice, first specify the lower and upper bound, which indicates the slice can take components from the given slice, beginning with the lower bound and the upper bound. It excludes the items from the upper bound above. As illustrated in the following example:

Syntax:

```
slicename[low:high]
```

This syntax will return a new slice.

Note that the lower bound is 0 by default, while the upper bound is set to the total number of items in the specified slice.

Example:

```
// Program to illustrate how to
// create slices from slice
package main
import "fmt"
func main() {
    // Creating s slice
    oRignAl_slice := []int{80, 20, 50, 10,
        54, 89, 70}
    // Creating the slices from the given slice
    var myslice1 = oRignAl_slice[1:5]
    myslice2 := oRignAl_slice[0:]
    myslice3 := oRignAl_slice[:6]
    myslice4 := oRignAl_slice[:]
    myslice5 := myslice3[2:4]
    // Display result
    fmt.Println("Original Slice:", oRignAl_slice)
    fmt.Println("New Slice 1:", myslice1)
    fmt.Println("New Slice 2:", myslice2)
    fmt.Println("New Slice 3:", myslice3)
    fmt.Println("New Slice 4:", myslice4)
    fmt.Println("New Slice 5:", myslice5)
}
```

Using the make() Function
We can also use the go library's make() function to generate a slice. This function has three input parameters: type, length, and capacity.

The capacity value is optional in this case. It returns a slice that references the underlying array and assigns an underlying array with a size equal to the given capacity. In most cases, the make() method produces an empty slice. In this context, empty slices have an empty array reference.

Syntax:

```
func make([]T, len, cap) []T
```

Example:

```go
// Program to illustrate how to create slices
// Using the make function
package main
import "fmt"

func main() {
    // Creating array of size 7 and slice this
array  till 4
    // and return the reference of the slice
    // Using make function
    var myslice1 = make([]int, 4, 7)
    fmt.Printf("Slice 1 = %v, \nlength = %d, \
ncapacity = %d\n",
                     myslice1, len(myslice1),
cap(myslice1))
    // Creating the another array of size 7
    // and return the reference of slice
    // Using the make function
    var myslice2 = make([]int, 7)
    fmt.Printf("Slice 2 = %v, \nlength = %d, \
ncapacity = %d\n",
                     myslice2, len(myslice2),
cap(myslice2))
}
```

How to Iterate over a Slice

It is possible to iterate across slice in the following ways:

Using the for loop

It is the easiest technique to iterate slices, as seen in the following example:

```go
// program to illustrate
// the iterating over a slice using for loop
package main
import "fmt"
func main() {
    // Creating slice
    myslice := []string{"This", "is", "the",
"example",
        "of", "Go", "language"}
    // Iterate using the for loop
    for x := 0; x < len(myslice); x++ {
        fmt.Println(myslice[x])
    }
}
```

Using Range in the for loop

Using range in for loop allows us to iterate across a slice. The index and element value may be obtained using range in for loop, as demonstrated in the following example:

```go
// Program to illustrate the iterating
// over a slice using range in for loop
package main
import "fmt"
func main() {
    // Creating a slice
    myslice := []string{"This", "is", "the", "example",
                                "of", "Go",
"programing"}
    // Iterate the slice using range in for loop
    for index, ele := range myslice {
        fmt.Printf("Index = %d and element = %s\n",
index+3, ele)
    }
}
```

Using a Blank Identifier in a for loop

If we don't want to retrieve the index value of the elements in the range for loop, we may use blank space(_) in place of the index variable, as illustrated in the following example:

```
// program to illustrate the iterating over
// a slice using a range in for loop without an index
package main
import "fmt"
func main() {
    // Creating slice
    myslice := []string{"This", "is", "the",
        "example", "of", "Go", "programing"}
    // Iterate the slice
    // using range in for loop without index
    for _, ele := range myslice {
        fmt.Printf("Element = %s\n", ele)
    }
}
```

Important Points about Slice

Zero Value Slice

In the Go programming language, we may build a nil slice that has no elements. As a result, the capacity and length of this slice are both 0. As seen in the following example, a nil slice does not include an array reference:

```
// Program to illustrate a zero value slice
package main
import "fmt"
func main() {
    // Creating zero value slice
    var myslice []string
    fmt.Printf("Length is = %d\n", len(myslice))
    fmt.Printf("Capacity is = %d ", cap(myslice))
}
```

Modifying Slices

Because slice is a reference type, it can refer to an underlying array. So, if we modify any elements in the slice, the changes should be reflected in the referenced array as well. In other words, if we make changes to the slice, the changes will be reflected in the array, as seen in the following example:

```
// Program to illustrate
// how to modify slice
package main
import "fmt"
func main() {
    // Creating zero value slice
    arry := [6]int{25, 86, 97, 33, 49, 21}
    slc := arry[0:4]
    // Before the modifying
    fmt.Println("Original_Array: ", arry)
    fmt.Println("Original_Slice: ", slc)
    // After the modification
    slc[0] = 10
    slc[1] = 100
    slc[2] = 1000
    fmt.Println("\nNew_Array: ", arr)
    fmt.Println("New_Slice: ", slc)
}
```

Slice Comparison

In slice, we can only use the == operator to determine whether a particular slice is nill or not. If we try to compare two slices using the == operator, we will get an error, as shown in the following example:

```
// Program to check if
// the slice is nil or not
package main
import "fmt"
func main() {
    // creating the slices
    st1 := []int{22, 38, 46}
    var st2 []int
    // If we try to run this commented
    // code compiler will give error
    /*st3:= []int{13, 55, 69}
      fmt.Println(st1==st3)
    */
```

```
    // Checking if the given slice is nil or not
    fmt.Println(st1 == nil)
    fmt.Println(st2 == nil)
}
```

Note: To compare two slices, use a range for loop to match each element, or use the DeepEqual function.

Multidimensional Slice

A multidimensional slice is similar to a multidimensional array, except that the slice does not include the size.

Example:

```
// Program to illustrate multi-dimensional slice
package main
import "fmt"
func main() {
    // Creating the multi-dimensional slice
    st1 := [][]int{{13, 39},
        {46, 57},
        {99, 30},
        {26, 76},
    }
    // Accessing the multi-dimensional slice
    fmt.Println("Slice 1 : ", st1)
    // Creating multi-dimensional slice
    st2 := [][]string{
        []string{"Hello", "for"},
        []string{"everyone", "HFE"},
        []string{"hfw", "hello"},
    }
    // Accessing the multi-dimensional slice
    fmt.Println("Slice 2 : ", st2)
}
```

Sorting of Slice

We may sort the elements in a slice in the Go programming language. The sort package is included in the Go language's standard library and offers several sorting techniques for sorting slices of ints, float64s, and strings.

These functions always sort the elements in ascending order accessible in the slice.

Example:

```go
// Program to illustrate how to sort
// elements present in the slice
package main
import (
    "fmt"
    "sort"
)
func main() {
    // Creating the Slice
    slc1 := []string{"C++", "Java", " Python ",
"Go", "Python"}
    slc2 := []int{35, 87, 13, 91, 34, 41, 86, 58,
69}
    fmt.Println("Before the sorting:")
    fmt.Println("Slice 1: ", slc1)
    fmt.Println("Slice 2: ", slc2)
    // Performing sort operation on the
    // slice using the sort function
    sort.Strings(slc1)
    sort.Ints(slc2)
    fmt.Println("\nAfter sorting:")
    fmt.Println("Slice 1: ", slc1)
    fmt.Println("Slice 2: ", slc2)

}
```

Slice Composite Literal

Slice and Composite Literal are the two words. Slice is a composite data type that, like an array, contains items of the same data type. The significant distinction between an array and a slice is that a slice's size may change dynamically, but an array cannot.

Values for arrays, structs, slices, and maps are constructed using composite literal. Each time they are evaluated, a new value is created. They are made up of the literal's type followed by a brace-bound list of items. After reading this, we will understand what a composite literal is, and we will be surprised that we already know.

Let's look at how to create a slice and use a composite literal:

```
// Program to show the slice composite literal
package main
import "fmt"
func main() {
    // Slice with the composite literal
    // Slice allows us to group together
    // the values of same type
    // here the type of values is int
    st1 := []int{53, 26, 19, 84}
    // displaying the values
    fmt.Println(st1)
}
```

We understand what is meant by the term "composite literal." As a result, composite literals are used to assign values or initialize arrays, slices, etc. These are often used to combine a collection of values of comparable sorts.

In GoLang, How Do We Sort a Slice of Ints?

Slice is a Go data structure that is more versatile, powerful, and convenient than an array. The slice is a variable-length sequence containing elements of the same kind; multiple components cannot be stored in the same slice.

The Go programming language allows us to order the slice's items based on their type. As a result, an int type slice is sorted using the below functions. Because these functions are specified in the sort package, we must import the sort package into our application to use them:

Ints

This function only sorts a slice of ints, and the elements in the slice are sorted in increasing order.

Syntax:

```
func Ints(slc []int)
```

In this case, slc represents a slice of ints. Let us illustrate this notion with an example:

```
// Program to demonstrate how
// to sort slice of ints
```

```go
package main
import (
    "fmt"
    "sort"
)
// the main function
func main() {
    // Creating, initializing slices
    // Using the shorthand declaration
    scl1 := []int{300, 500, 200, 300, 400, 700, 800}
    scl2 := []int{-13, 267, -54, 69, 0, 22, -4}
    // Displaying the slices
    fmt.Println("Slices(Before):")
    fmt.Println("Slice 1: ", scl1)
    fmt.Println("Slice 2: ", scl2)
    // Sortingslice of ints
    // Using Ints function
    sort.Ints (scl1)
    sort.Ints (scl2)
    // Displaying result
    fmt.Println("\nSlices(After):")
    fmt.Println("Slice 1 : ", scl1)
    fmt.Println("Slice 2 : ",scl2)
}
```

IntsAreSorted

This function determines whether the supplied slice of ints is sorted (in increasing order) or not. If the slice is in sorted form, this function returns true; otherwise, it returns false.

Syntax:

```go
func IntsAreSorted(scl []int) bool
```

In this case, scl represents a slice of ints. Let us illustrate this notion with an example:

```go
// Program to demonstrate how to check
// whether a given slice of ints is in
// sorted the form or not
package main
import (
```

```
    "fmt"
    "sort"
)
// the main function
func main() {
    // Creating, initializing slices
    // Using the shorthand declaration
    scl1 := []int{200, 100, 800, 300, 400, 500, 700}
    scl2 := []int{-13, 547, -24, 97, 0, 18, -5}
    // Displaying the slices
    fmt.Println("Slices:")
    fmt.Println("Slice 1: ", scl1)
    fmt.Println("Slice 2: ", scl2)
    // Checking slice is in sorted form or not
    // Using IntsAreSorted function
    rest1 := sort.IntsAreSorted(scl1)
    rest2 := sort.IntsAreSorted(scl2)
    // Displaying result
    fmt.Println("\nResult:")
    fmt.Println("Is Slice 1 is sorted?: ", rest1)
    fmt.Println("Is Slice 2 is sorted?: ", rest2)
}
```

In GoLang, How Can You Trim a Slice of Bytes?

Slice is a Go data structure that is more versatile, powerful, and convenient than an array. The slice is a variable-length sequence containing elements of the same kind; multiple components cannot be stored in the same slice.

Trim() method in the Go slice of bytes allows us to trim all the beginning and trailing UTF-8-encoded code points from the specified slice.

This method produces a subslice of the original slice by removing all leading and trailing UTF-8-encoded code points from the provided string. If the provided bytes slice does not contain the required string, this method returns the original slice with no changes. Because it is specified in the bytes package, we must import the bytes package in our application to use the Trim function.

Syntax:

```
func Trim(ori_slice []byte, cut_string string) []byte
```

The original slice of bytes is represented by ori_slice, and cut_string represents a string that we want to trim in the given slice. Let us examine this notion using the following examples:

First example:

```
// Program to demonstrate the concept of trim in
the slice of bytes
package main
import (
    "bytes"
    "fmt"
)
func main() {
    // Creating, initializing
    // the slice of bytes
    // Using the shorthand declaration
    slice_1 := []byte{'!', '!', 'H', 'e', 'e',
'l', 'o', 'o',
                    'o', 'r', 'W', 'o', 'r', 'l',
'd', '#', '#'}
    slice_2 := []byte{'*', '*', 'G', 'r', 'a',
'p', 'e', '^', '^'}
    slice_3 := []byte{'%', 'h', 'e', 'l', 'l',
'o', '%'}
    // Displaying slices
    fmt.Println("The Original Slice:")
    fmt.Printf("Slice 1: %s", slice_1)
    fmt.Printf("\nSlice 2: %s", slice_2)
    fmt.Printf("\nSlice 3: %s", slice_3)
    // Trimming the specified leading
    // and trailing Unicodes points
    // from given slice of bytes
    // Using Trim function
    rest1 := bytes.Trim(slice_1, "!#")
    rest2 := bytes.Trim(slice_2, "*^")
    rest3 := bytes.Trim(slice_3, "@")
    // Display results
    fmt.Printf("New Slice:\n")
    fmt.Printf("\nSlice 1: %s", rest1)
    fmt.Printf("\nSlice 2: %s", rest2)
    fmt.Printf("\nSlice 3: %s", rest3)
}
```

Second example:

```go
// Program to demonstrate the concept of trim in
the slice of bytes
package main
import (
    "bytes"
    "fmt"
)
func main() {
    // Creating, trimming the slice of bytes
    // Using the Trim function
    rest1 := bytes.Trim([]byte("****Welcome to
GoWorld****"), "*")
    rest2 := bytes.Trim([]byte("!!!!Learning how
to trim slice of bytes@@@@"), "!@")
    rest3 := bytes.Trim([]byte("^^hello&&"), "$")
    // Display  results
    fmt.Printf("Final Slice:\n")
    fmt.Printf("\nSlice 1: %s", rest1)
    fmt.Printf("\nSlice 2: %s", rest2)
    fmt.Printf("\nSlice 3: %s", rest3)
}
```

How Can You Split a Slice of Bytes in GoLang?

Slice is a Go data structure that is more versatile, powerful, and convenient than an array. The slice is a variable-length sequence containing elements of the same kind; multiple components cannot be stored in the same slice.

We may split the provided slice of bytes in Go using the Split() method. This method divides a byte slice into all subslices divided by the provided separator and returns a slice containing all of these subslices. Because it is specified in the bytes package, we must import the bytes package in our program to use the Split function.

Syntax:

```go
func Split(o_slice, sep []byte) [][]byte
```

In this case, o_slice is the bytes slice, and sep is the separator. If the sep is empty, it will divide after each UTF-8 sequence. Let us examine this notion using the following examples:

First example:

```go
// Program to illustrate the concept
// of splitting a slice of bytes
package main

import (
    "bytes"
    "fmt"
)
func main() {
    // Creating, initializing the slice of bytes
    // Using the shorthand declaration
    slice_1 := []byte{'!', '!', 'H', 'e', 'l',
'l', 'o',
        'f', 'o', 'r', 'W', 'o', 'r', 'l', 'd',
'#', '#'}
    slice_2 := []byte{'G', 'r', 'a', 'p', 'e'}
    slice_3 := []byte{'%', 'h', '%', 'e', '%',
'l',
                      '%', 'l', '%', 'o', '%'}
    // Displaying slices
    fmt.Println("Original Slice:")
    fmt.Printf("Slice 1: %s", slice_1)
    fmt.Printf("\nSlice 2: %s", slice_2)
    fmt.Printf("\nSlice 3: %s", slice_3)
    // Splitting slice of bytes
    // Using the Split function
    rest1 := bytes.Split(slice_1, []byte("eek"))
    rest2 := bytes.Split(slice_2, []byte(""))
    rest3 := bytes.Split(slice_3, []byte("%"))
    // Display results
    fmt.Printf("\n\nAfter splitting:")
    fmt.Printf("\nSlice 1: %s", rest1)
    fmt.Printf("\nSlice 2: %s", rest2)
    fmt.Printf("\nSlice 3: %s", rest3)
}
```

Second example:

```go
// Program to illustrate the concept
// of splitting a slice of bytes
package main
```

```go
import (
    "bytes"
    "fmt"
)
func main() {
    // Creating, Splitting the slice of bytes
    // Using the Split function
    rest1 := bytes.Split([]byte("****Welcome, to,
Tutorial****"),

[]byte(","))
    rest2 := bytes.Split([]byte("Learning x how x
to x trim x a x slice of bytes"),

[]byte("x"))
    rest3 := bytes.Split([]byte("Helloworld,
world"), []byte(""))
    rest4 := bytes.Split([]byte(""), []byte(","))
    // Display results
    fmt.Printf("Final Value:\n")
    fmt.Printf("\nSlice 1: %s", rest1)
    fmt.Printf("\nSlice 2: %s", rest2)
    fmt.Printf("\nSlice 3: %s", rest3)
    fmt.Printf("\nSlice 4: %s", rest4)
}
```

STRINGS

Strings in Go differ from those in other languages such as Java, C++, Python, etc. It is a string of variable-width characters, each represented by one or more bytes encoded with UTF-8. In other terms, strings are an immutable chain of arbitrary bytes (including zero-valued bytes), or strings are a read-only slice of bytes whose bytes may be expressed in Unicode text using UTF-8 encoding.

Because of UTF-8 encoding, a GoLang string may include content that is a mash-up of every language in the world without causing confusion or limiting the page. Strings are typically enclosed in double-quotes''', as shown in the following example:

```go
// Program to illustrate
// how to create strings
package main
import "fmt"
```

```go
func main() {
    // Creating, initializing a
    // variable with a string
    // Using the shorthand declaration
    My_value_1 := "Welcome to Home"
    // Using the var keyword
    var My_value_2 string
    My_value_2 = "World"
    // Displaying the strings
    fmt.Println("String 1: ", My_value_1)
    fmt.Println("String 2: ", My_value_2)
}
```

String Literals

String literals are formed in two ways in the Go programming language.

Using Double Quotes("")

The string literals, in this case, are produced using double quotes(""). This sort of string can contain escape characters, as described in the following table, but it cannot extend several lines. String literals of this kind are commonly used in GoLang programming.

Escape Character	Description
\\	Backslash
\000	Unicode character with given 3-digit 8-bit octal code point
\'	Single quote('). It is only allowed inside the character literals
\"	Double quote("). It is only allowed inside the interpreted string literals
\a	ASCII bell
\b	ASCII backspace
\f	ASCII formfeed
\n	ASCII linefeed
\r	ASCII carriage return
\t	ASCII tab
\uhhhh	Unicode character with given 4-digit 16-bit hex code point
	Unicode character with given 8-digit 32-bit hex code point
\v	ASCII vertical tab
\xhh	Unicode character with given 2-digit 8-bit hex code point

Using backticks("")

String literals are formed using backticks("") and are also known as raw literals in this context. Raw literals do not allow escape characters, span many lines, and contain any other characters than the backtick. It is commonly used for producing multiline messages, regular expressions, and HTML.

Example:

```
// Program to illustrate string literals
package main
import "fmt"
func main() {
    // Creating, initializing a
    // variable with string literal
    // Using the double-quote
    My_value_1 := "Welcome to World"
    // Adding escape character
    My_value_2 := "Welcome!\nWorld "
    // Using backticks
    My_value_3 := 'Hello!Everyone'
    // Adding the escape character
    // in the raw literals
    My_value_4 := 'Hello!\nGeeksforGeeks'
    // Displaying the strings
    fmt.Println("The String 1: ", My_value_1)
    fmt.Println("The String 2: ", My_value_2)
    fmt.Println("The String 3: ", My_value_3)
    fmt.Println("The String 4: ", My_value_4)
}
```

Important Points about Strings

Strings Are Immutable

Strings are immutable in Go. Once a string is formed, it isn't easy to modify the value. Strings, in other words, are read-only. If we attempt to alter something, the compiler will raise an error.

Example:

```
// Program to illustrate
// the string are immutable
package main
import "fmt"
// the main function
func main() {
```

```
    // Creating, initializing a string
    // using the shorthand declaration
    mystr := "Welcome to World"
    fmt.Println("String:", mystr)
    /* if we trying to change
            the value of string
            then compiler will
            throw error, i.e,
         cannot assign to mystr[1]
       mystry[1] = 'G'
       fmt.Println("String:", mystry)
    */
}
```

How to Iterate over a String

Use the for rang loop to iterate through a string. This loop may iterate across a string's Unicode code point.

Syntax:

```
for index, chr:= range str{
    // Statement
}
```

Here, the index is a variable that stores the first byte of a UTF-8 encoded code point, chr is a variable that stores the characters of the provided string, and str is a string.

Example:

```
// Program to illustrate how
// to iterate over string
// using the for range loop
package main
import "fmt"
// the main function
func main() {
    // String as a range in for loop
    for index, st := range "Helloeveryone" {
                fmt.Printf("Index number of %c is
%d\n", st, index)
    }
}
```

How to Access an Individual Byte of the String
We can access each byte of the provided text because it is a byte string.

Example:

```
// Program to illustrate how to
// access bytes of the string
package main
import "fmt"
// Main function
func main() {
    // Creating, initializing a string
    str := "Welcome to World"
    // Accessing the bytes of the given string
    for x := 0; x < len(str); x++ {
        fmt.Printf("\nCharacter = %c Bytes = %v",
str, str)
    }
}
```

How to Make a String from a Slice of Bytes
In Go, we can make a string from a slice of bytes.

Example:

```
package main
import (
    "fmt"
    "reflect"
    "strings"
)
func main() {
    stry1 := []string{"Drum", "of", "India", "On",
"Dec"}
    fmt.Println(stry1)
    fmt.Println(reflect.TypeOf(stry1))

    stry2 := strings.Join(stry1, " ")
    fmt.Println(stry2)
    fmt.Println(reflect.TypeOf(stry2))
    stry3 := strings.Join(stry1, ", ")
    fmt.Println(stry3)
    fmt.Println(reflect.TypeOf(stry3))
}
```

How Can We Determine the Length of a String in GoLang?

We can find the length of a string in GoLang by utilizing two functions: len() and RuneCountInString (). The UTF-8 package includes the RuneCountInString() method, which returns the total rune in the string. And the len() method returns the string's length in bytes.

Example:

```go
// Program to illustrate how to
// find the length of the string
package main
import (
    "fmt"
    "unicode/utf8"
)
// the main function
func main() {
    // Creating, initializing a string
    // using the shorthand declaration
    mystr := "Welcome to Everyone???"
    // Finding length of the string
    // Using len() function
    length1 := len(mystr)
    // Using the RuneCountInString() function
    length2 := utf8.RuneCountInString(mystr)
    // Displaying length of the string
    fmt.Println("string:", mystr)
    fmt.Println("Length 1:", length1)
    fmt.Println("Length 2:", length2)
}
```

In GoLang, How Do We Trim a String?

Strings in Go differ from those in other languages such as Java, C++, Python, etc. It is a string of variable-width characters, each represented by one or more bytes encoded with UTF-8. We may trim a string in various ways by using the following listed methods. These functions are specified in the strings package; thus, we must import the strings package in your application to use them.

Trim

This function trims the text by removing all of the leading and trailing Unicode code points given in this function.

Syntax:

```
func Trim(str string, cutstr string) string
```

In this case, str represents the current string, and cutstr represents the elements in the specified string that we want to remove.

Example:

```
// Program to illustrate
// how to trim string
package main
import (
    "fmt"
    "strings"
)
// the main method
func main() {
    // Creating, initializing string
    // Using the shorthand declaration
    stry1 := "!!Welcome to Everyone !!"
    stry2 := "@@This is the example of Golang$$"
    // Displaying strings
    fmt.Println("Strings before the trimming:")
    fmt.Println("String 1: ", stry1)
    fmt.Println("String 2:", stry2)
    // Trimming given strings
    // Using Trim() function
    rest1 := strings.Trim(stry1, "!")
    rest2 := strings.Trim(stry2, "@$")
    // Displaying results
    fmt.Println("\nStrings after the trimming:")
    fmt.Println("Result 1: ", rest1)
    fmt.Println("Result 2:", rest2)
}
```

TrimLeft

TrimLeft function is used to trim the string's Unicode code points on the left-hand side (given in the function).

Syntax:

```
func TrimLeft(str string, cutstr string) string
```

In this case, str represents the current string, and cutstr represents the left-hand side elements of the specified string that we want to trim.

Example:

```
// Program to illustrate how to
// trim the left-hand side elements
// from string
package main
import (
    "fmt"
    "strings"
)
// the main method
func main() {
    // Creating, initializing string
    // Using the shorthand declaration
    stry1 := "!!Welcome to Everyone **"
    stry2 := "@@This is the example of Golang$$"
    // Displaying the strings
    fmt.Println("Strings before trimming:")
    fmt.Println("String 1: ", stry1)
    fmt.Println("String 2:", stry2)
    // Trimming the given strings
    // Using the TrimLeft() function
    rest1 := strings.TrimLeft(str1, "!*")
    rest2 := strings.TrimLeft(str2, "@")
      // Displaying results
    fmt.Println("\nStrings after trimming:")
    fmt.Println("Result 1: ", rest1)
    fmt.Println("Result 2:", rest2)
}
```

TrimRight
This function trims the string's right-hand side (given in the function) Unicode code points.

Syntax:

```
func TrimRight(str string, cutstr string) string
```

In this case, str represents the current string, and cutstr represents the right-hand side components of the specified string that we want to trim.

Example:

```
// Program to illustrate how to
// trim the right-hand side elements
// from string
package main
import (
    "fmt"
    "strings"
)
// the main method
func main() {
    // Creating, initializing the
    // string using the shorthand declaration
    stry1 := "!!Welcome to Everyone **"
    stry2 := "@@This is the example of Golang$$"
    // Displaying the strings
    fmt.Println("Strings before the trimming:")
    fmt.Println("String 1: ", stry1)
    fmt.Println("String 2:", stry2)
    // Trimming given strings
    // Using the TrimRight() function
    rest1 := strings.TrimRight(stry1, "!*")
    rest2 := strings.TrimRight(stry2, "$")
    // Displaying results
    fmt.Println("\nStrings after trimming:")
    fmt.Println("Result 1: ", rest1)
    fmt.Println("Result 2:", rest2)
}
```

TrimSpace

This method removes all leading and trailing white space from the given string.

Syntax:

```
func TrimSpace(str string) string
```

Example:

```
// Program to illustrate how to
// trim the white space from string
package main
import (
    "fmt"
    "strings"
)
// the main method
func main() {
    // Creating, initializing string
    // Using the shorthand declaration
    stry1 := "   **Welcome to Everyone**   "
    stry2 := "  ##This is the example of Golang##   "
    // Displaying the strings
    fmt.Println("Strings before the trimming:")
    fmt.Println(stry1, stry2)
    // Trimming the white space from given strings
    // Using TrimSpace() function
    rest1 := strings.TrimSpace(stry1)
    rest2 := strings.TrimSpace(stry2)
      // Displaying results
    fmt.Println("\nStrings after the trimming:")
    fmt.Println(rest1, rest2)
}
```

TrimSuffix

This method removes the string's trailing suffix. If the provided string does not include the specified suffix string, this method returns the original string unaltered.

Syntax:

```
func TrimSuffix(str, suffstr string) string
```

The original string is represented by str, while the suffix string is represented by suffstr.

Example:

```
// Program to illustrate how to
// trim suffix string from
```

```go
// the given string
package main
import (
    "fmt"
    "strings"
)
// the main method
func main() {
    // Creating, initializing string
    // Using the shorthand declaration
    stry1 := "Welcome, Everyone"
    stry2 := "This is the, example of Golang"
    // Displaying the strings
    fmt.Println("Strings before the trimming:")
    fmt.Println("String 1: ", stry1)
    fmt.Println("String 2:", stry2)
    // Trimming the suffix string from given strings
    // Using the TrimSuffix() function
    rest1 := strings.TrimSuffix(str1, "Helloworld")
    rest2 := strings.TrimSuffix(str2, "Helloo")
    // Displaying results
    fmt.Println("\nStrings after the trimming:")
    fmt.Println("Result 1: ", rest1)
    fmt.Println("Result 2:", rest2)
}
```

TrimPrefix

This method removes the string's leading prefix. If the provided string does not include the requested prefix string, this method returns the original string unaltered.

Syntax:

```go
func TrimPrefix(str, suffstr string) string
```

The original string is represented by str, while the prefix string is represented by suffstr.

Example:

```go
// Program to illustrate how to
// trim prefix string from
```

```
// the given string
package main
import (
    "fmt"
    "strings"
)
// the Main method
func main() {
    // Creating, initializing string
    // Using the shorthand declaration
    stry1 := "Welcome, Everyone"
    stry2 := "This is the, example of Golang"
    // Displaying the strings
    fmt.Println("Strings before the trimming:")
    fmt.Println("String 1: ", stry1)
    fmt.Println("String 2: ", stry2)
    // Trimming the prefix string from given
strings
    // Using the TrimPrefix() function
    rest1 := strings.TrimPrefix(str1, "Hello")
    rest2 := strings.TrimPrefix(str2, "World")
    // Displaying results
    fmt.Println("\nStrings after the trimming:")
    fmt.Println("Result 1: ", rest1)
    fmt.Println("Result 2: ", rest2)
}
```

In GoLang, How Do We Split a String?

Strings in Go differ from those in other languages such as Java, C++, Python, etc. It is a string of variable-width characters, each represented by one or more bytes encoded with UTF-8. With the aid of the following functions, we can split a string into a slice in Go strings. Because these functions are specified in the strings package, we must import the strings package in our program to use them:

Split

This function splits the string into all substrings separated by the separator specified and returns a slice containing these substrings.

Syntax:

```
func Split(str, sep string) []string
```

The string str is used here, and the separator sep is used. If str does not include the given sep and sep is not empty, it will return a slice of length 1 that solely contains str. If the sep parameter is left empty, it will divide after each UTF-8 sequence. Alternatively, if both str and sep are empty, it will produce an empty slice.

Example:

```
// Program to demonstrate how to split a string
package main
import (
    "fmt"
    "strings"
)
// the main function
func main() {
    // Creating, initializing the strings
    stry1 := "Welcome, to the, our channel,
Helloeveryone"
    stry2 := "My dog name is Dollar"
    stry3 := "I like to play Ludo"
    // Displaying the strings
    fmt.Println("String 1: ", stry1)
    fmt.Println("String 2: ", stry2)
    fmt.Println("String 3: ", stry3)
    // Splitting given strings
    // Using the Split() function
    rest1 := strings.Split(stry1, ",")
    rest2 := strings.Split(stry2, "")
    rest3 := strings.Split(stry3, "!")
    rest4 := strings.Split("", "Helloeveryone,
hello")
    // Displaying result
    fmt.Println("\nResult 1: ", rest1)
    fmt.Println("Result 2: ", rest2)
    fmt.Println("Result 3: ", rest3)
    fmt.Println("Result 4: ", rest4)
}
```

SplitAfter
Splits a string into all substrings after each instance of the provided separator and returns a slice containing these substrings.

Syntax:

```
func SplitAfter(str, sep string) []string
```

The string str is used here, and the separator sep is used. If str does not include the given sep and sep is not empty, it will return a slice of length 1 that solely contains str. If the sep parameter is left empty, it will divide after each UTF-8 sequence. Alternatively, if both str and sep are empty, it will produce an empty slice.

Example:

```
// Program to demonstrate how to split a string
package main
import (
    "fmt"
    "strings"
)
// the main function
func main() {
    // Creating, initializing the strings
    stry1 := "Welcome, to the, online session,
Helloeveryone"
    stry2 := "My cat name is puffi"
    stry3 := "I like to play chess"
    // Displaying the strings
    fmt.Println("String 1: ", stry1)
    fmt.Println("String 2: ", stry2)
    fmt.Println("String 3: ", stry3)
    // Splitting given strings
    // Using the SplitAfter() function
    rest1 := strings.SplitAfter(str1, ",")
    rest2 := strings.SplitAfter(str2, "")
    rest3 := strings.SplitAfter(str3, "!")
    rest4 := strings.SplitAfter("",
"Helloeveryone, Hello")
    // Displaying result
    fmt.Println("\nResult 1: ", rest1)
    fmt.Println("Result 2: ", rest2)
    fmt.Println("Result 3: ", rest3)
    fmt.Println("Result 4: ", rest4)
}
```

SplitAfterN

Splits a string into all substrings after each use of the provided separator and returns a slice containing these substrings.

Syntax:

```
func SplitAfterN(str, sep string, m int) []string
```

In this case, str is the string, sep is the separator, and m is the number of substrings to return. If m>0, it will return at most m substrings, with the final string substring not splitting. If m == zero, it will return nil. If m<0, it returns all substrings.

Example:

```
// Program to demonstrate how to split a string
package main
import (
    "fmt"
    "strings"
)
// the main function
func main() {
    // Creating, initializing the strings
    stry1 := "Welcome, to the, online session,
Helloeveryone"
    stry2 := "My cat name is puffi"
    stry3 := "I like to play chess"
    // Displaying strings
    fmt.Println("String 1: ", stry1)
    fmt.Println("String 2: ", stry2)
    fmt.Println("String 3: ", stry3)
    // Splitting given strings
    // Using SplitAfterN() function
    rest1 := strings.SplitAfterN(stry1, ",", 2)
    rest2 := strings.SplitAfterN(stry2, "", 4)
    rest3 := strings.SplitAfterN(stry3, "!", 1)
    rest4 := strings.SplitAfterN("",
 "Helloeveryone, hello", 3)
    // Displaying result
    fmt.Println("\nResult 1: ", rest1)
    fmt.Println("Result 2: ", rest2)
```

```
        fmt.Println("Result 3: ", rest3)
        fmt.Println("Result 4: ", rest4)
}
```

In GoLang, There Are Several Ways to Compare Strings

The string in Go is an immutable chain of arbitrary bytes encoded using UTF-8 encoding. We have two options for comparing strings to each other:

Making Use of Comparison Operators

Go strings allow comparison operators such as ==, !=, >=, <=, <, >. The == and != operators are used to determine if the given strings are equal, while the >=, <=, <, > operators determine the lexical order. The outcomes of these operators are of the Boolean type, which means that if the condition is met. It will return true; otherwise, false.

First example:

```
// Program to illustrate the concept
// of == and != operator with the strings
package main
import "fmt"
// the main function
func main() {
    // Creating, initializing strings
    // using the shorthand declaration
    stry1 := "Hello"
    stry2 := "Helo"
    stry3 := "Helloeveryone"
    stry4 := "Hello"
    // Checking string are equal
    // or not using == operator
    res1 := str1 == str2
    res2 := str2 == str3
    res3 := str3 == str4
    res4 := str1 == str4
    fmt.Println("Result 1: ", res1)
    fmt.Println("Result 2: ", res2)
    fmt.Println("Result 3: ", res3)
    fmt.Println("Result 4: ", res4)
    // Checking the string are not equal
    // using != operator
```

```
    res5 := str1 != str2
    res6 := str2 != str3
    res7 := str3 != str4
    res8 := str1 != str4
    fmt.Println("\nResult 5: ", res5)
    fmt.Println("Result 6: ", res6)
    fmt.Println("Result 7: ", res7)
    fmt.Println("Result 8: ", res8)
}
```

Second example:

```
// Program to illustrate concept
// of comparison operator with the strings
package main
import "fmt"
// the main function
func main() {
    // Creating, initializing
    // slice of string using
    // the shorthand declaration
    myslice := []string{"Hello", "Hello",
                    "hfw", "HFW", "from"}
    fmt.Println("Slice: ", myslice)
    // Using the comparison operator
    result1 := "HFW" > "Hello"
    fmt.Println("Result 1: ", result1)
    result2 := "HFW" < "hello"
    fmt.Println("Result 2: ", result2)
    result3 := "Hello" >= "from"
    fmt.Println("Result 3: ", result3)
    result4 := "Hello" <= "from"
    fmt.Println("Result 4: ", result4)
    result5 := "Hello" == "Hello"
    fmt.Println("Result 5: ", result5)
    result6 := "Hello" != "from"
    fmt.Println("Result 6: ", result6)
}
```

Using Compare() Method

We may also compare two strings using the strings package's built-in function Compare(). After comparing two strings lexicographically, this method produces an integer value. The values returned are as follows:

```
Return 0, if stry1 == stry2.
Return 1, if stry1 > stry2.
Return -1, if stry1 < stry2.
```

Syntax:

```
func Compare(stry1, stry2 string) int
```

Example:

```
// Program to illustrate how to compare
// the string using compare() function
package main
import (
    "fmt"
    "strings"
)
func main() {
    // Comparing string using the Compare function
    fmt.Println(strings.Compare("hfw", "Hello"))
    fmt.Println(strings.Compare("Helloeveryone",
                                "Hello"))
    fmt.Println(strings.Compare("Hello", " HFW"))
    fmt.Println(strings.Compare("HelLo", "HelLo"))
}
```

MAPS

A map is a strong, inventive, and flexible data structure in the Go programming language. Maps in GoLang language are a collection of key-value pairs that are not ordered. It is commonly used because it allows quick lookups and values that may be retrieved, updated, or delete using keys.

- It's a hash table reference.

- It is inexpensive to pass due to its reference type; for example, on a 64-bit processor, it requires 8 bytes, while on a 32-bit machine, it takes 4 bytes.

- A key in a map must be unique and always of the type that is compared using the == operator or the type that supports the != operator.

As a result, most built-in types, such as int, float64, rune, string, similar array and structure, pointer, and so on, may be used as keys. Data types such as slice and noncomparable arrays and structs and custom data types that are not comparable are not used as map keys.

- Values in maps are not unique like keys and can be of any type such as int, float64, string, rune, pointer, reference type, map type, etc.

- The Keys and values must be of same type; various keys and values in the same maps are not permitted. However, the type of key and type values might differ.

- A hash table, hash map, unordered map, dictionary, or associative array are other maps' names.

- We can only add value to a map after it has been initialized. If we add value to an uninitialized map, the compiler will give an error.

How Do We Create and Initialize Maps?

Maps in the Go programming language may be created and initialized in two ways:

Simple

We may use this way to construct and initialize a map without using the make() function:

1. **Creating a Map:** Using the following syntax, we can easily create a map:

```
// Empty map
map[KeyType]ValueType{}
// Map with the keyvalue pair
map[KeyType]ValueType{key1: value1, ..., keyN:
valueN}
```

Example:

```
var mymap map[int]string
```

The zero value of a map in maps is nil, and a nil map does not include any keys. If we insert a key-value pair into the nil map, the compiler will report a runtime error.

2. **Using map literals to initialize the map:** Map literals are the simplest way to populate a map with data; separate the key-value pair with a colon, and the last trailing colon is required; otherwise, the compiler will generate an error.

Example:

```go
// Program to illustrate how to
// create, initialize maps
package main
import "fmt"
func main() {
    // Creating, initializing empty map
    // Using the var keyword
    var map_1 map[int]int
    // Checking if map is nil or not
    if map_1 == nil {
        fmt.Println("True")
    } else {
        fmt.Println("False")
    }
    // Creating, initializing a map
    // Using the shorthand declaration and
    // using the map literals
    map_2 := map[int]string{
                90: "Duck",
                91: "Cow",
                92: "Cat",
                93: "Bird",
                94: "Boat",
    }
    fmt.Println("Map-2: ", map_2)
}
```

Using the make() Function

We can also create a map using the make() function. This function is an inbuilt function, and in this method, we need to pass the type of the map and return an initialized map.

Syntax:

```go
make(map[KeyType]ValueType, initial_Capacity)
make(map[KeyType]ValueType)
```

Example:

```
// Program to illustrate how to
// create, initialize a map
// Using the make() function
package main
import "fmt"
func main() {
    // Creating map
    // Using the make() function
    var Mymap = make(map[float64]string)
    fmt.Println(Mymap)
     // As we know that make() function always
returns a map which is initialized
    // we can add values in it
    Mymap[1.3] = "Ridhi"
    Mymap[1.5] = "Sunita"
    fmt.Println(Mymap)
}
```

Important Considerations

How Do We Iterate over a Map?

We may use the range for loop to iterate over a map. Because the map is an unordered collection, the value of this loop may vary.

Example:

```
// Program to illustrate how
// to iterate map using for rang loop
package main
 import "fmt"
// the main function
func main() {
    // Creating, initializing a map
    m_a_p := map[int]string{
        90: "Duck",
        91: "Cow",
        92: "Cat",
        93: "Bird",
        94: "Dog",
    }
    // Iterating the map using for rang loop
```

```
    for id, pet := range m_a_p {
        fmt.Println(id, pet)
    }
}
```

How to Add Key-Value Pairs to the Map
In maps, we may add key-value pairs to the initialized map using the following syntax:

```
map-name[key]=value
```

If we try to add key that already exists in a map, it will simply override or update value of that key with the new value.

Example:

```
// Program to illustrate how to add
 key-value pair in the map using make() function
package main
import "fmt"
// the main function
func main() {
    // Creating, initializing a map
    m_a_p := map[int]string{
        90: "Duck",
        91: "Cow",
        92: "Dog",
        93: "Cat",
        94: "Rabbit",
    }
    fmt.Println("Original map: ", m_a_p)
    // Adding the new key-value pairs in the map
    m_a_p[95] = "Parrot"
    m_a_p[96] = "Crow"
    fmt.Println("Map after adding the new key-
value pair:\n", m_a_p)
    // Updating the values of map
    m_a_p[91] = "PIG"
    m_a_p[93] = "MONKEY"
    fmt.Println("\nMap after updating the values
of map:\n", m_a_p)
}
```

How to Retrieve the Value Associated with a Key in a Map
In maps, use the following syntax to obtain a value using a key:

```
map_name [key]
```

If key does not exist in the given map, it will return its zero value, i.e., nil. And if the key is found in the given map, it will return the value associated with that key.

Example:

```
// Program to illustrate how to
// retrieve the value of key
package main
import "fmt"
// the ain function
func main() {
    // Creating, initializing a map
    m_a_p := map[int]string{
        90: "Duck",
        91: "Cow",
        92: "Cat",
        93: "Dog",
        94: "Rabbit",
    }
    fmt.Println("Original map: ", m_a_p)
    // Retrieving values with help of keys
    value_1 := m_a_p[91]
    value_2 := m_a_p[92]
    fmt.Println("Value of key[91]: ", value_1)
    fmt.Println("Value of key[92]: ", value_2)
}
```

How to Check If the Key Is Present on the Map
In maps, we may use the following syntax to determine whether or not a particular key exists:

Syntax:

```
// With the value
// It will give the value, check the result
value, checkvariablename:= mapname [key]
```

or

```
// Without the value using the blank identifier
// It will only give check result
_, checkvariablename := mapname[key]
```

If the value of the checkvariablename is true, the key exists in the given map; if the value of the checkvariablename is false, the key does not exist in the given map.

Example:

```
// Program to illustrate how to
// check key is available or not
package main
import "fmt"
// the main function
func main() {
    // Creating. initializing a map
    m_a_p := map[int]string{
        90: "Cow",
        91: "Cat",
        92: "Duck",
        93: "Dog",
        94: "Rabbit",
    }
    fmt.Println("Original map: ", m_a_p)
    // Checking key is available
  or not in the m_a_p map
    pet_name, ok := m_a_p[90]
    fmt.Println("\nThe Key present or not:", ok)
    fmt.Println("The Value:", pet_name)
    // Using the blank identifier
    _, ok1 := m_a_p[92]
    fmt.Println("\nThe Key present or not:", ok1)
}
```

How to Remove a Key from a Map

The delete() method in maps allows us to delete the key existing in the map. It is a built-in function that returns no value and does nothing if the key does not exist in the specified map. Simply pass the map and key that we want to remove from the map to this method.

Syntax:

```
delete(mapname, key)
```

Example:

```
// Program to illustrate how to delete key
package main
import "fmt"
// the main function
func main() {
    // Creating, initializing a map
    m_a_p := map[int]string{
        90: "Duck",
        91: "Cow",
        92: "Cat",
        93: "Dog",
        94: "Rabbit",
    }
    fmt.Println("Original map: ", m_a_p)
    // Deleting keys
    // Using the delete function
    delete(m_a_p, 91)
    delete(m_a_p, 92)
    fmt.Println("Map after deletion: ", m_a_p)
}
```

Map Modification

As we all know, maps are of the reference kind. As a result, when we assign an existing map to a new variable, both maps relate to the same underlying data structure. As a result, when we update one map, it will be reflected in another.

Example:

```
// Program to illustrate the
// modification concept in map
package main
import "fmt"
```

```
// the main function
func main() {
    // Creating, initializing a map
    m_a_p := map[int]string{
        90: "Duck",
        91: "Cow",
        92: "Cat",
        93: "Duck",
        94: "Rabbit",
    }
    fmt.Println("Original map: ", m_a_p)
    // Assigned map into a new variable
    new_map := m_a_p
    // Perform the modification in new_map
    new_map[96] = "Monkey"
    new_map[98] = "Donkey"
    // Display after modification
    fmt.Println("The New map: ", new_map)
    fmt.Println("\nModification done in old
map:\n", m_a_p)
}
```

In this chapter, we covered Arrays. We also discussed Slices and Maps with their relevant syntax and example.

CHAPTER 7

Functions and Recursion

IN THIS CHAPTER

➤ Returning multiple values

➤ Variadic functions

➤ Closure

➤ Recursion

➤ Defer, panic, and recover

Chapter 6 covered structures, array, slices, and maps. In this chapter, we will discuss returning multiple values, variadic functions, and closure. We will also cover recursion.

Go LANGUAGE FUNCTIONS

Functions are often the blocks of code or statements in a program that allows the user to reuse the same code, saving memory, saving time, and, most significantly, improving code readability. A function is, in essence, a set of statements that execute a given task and provide the outcome to the caller. A function can also carry out a specific task without returning any results.

Function Declaration

A function declaration is a method of constructing a function.

DOI: 10.1201/9781003310457-7

Syntax:

```
func function-name(Parameterlist)(Returntype){
    // function body
}
```

The following are included in the function's declaration:

- **func:** It is a keyword in the Go programming language used to define a function.

- **function-name:** This is the function's name.

- **Parameterlist:** It specifies the name and type of function arguments.

- **Returntype:** This parameter is optional and contains the types of values that the function returns. If we're going to utilize return type in our function, we'll need to include a return statement.

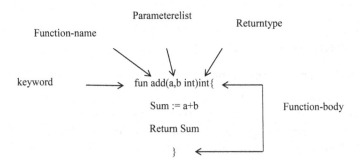

Function Calling

When a user wants to perform a function, they invoke it or call it. To use the function's capabilities, it must be invoked. As illustrated in the sample below, we have a function named area() with two parameters. We now call this function by its name in the main function, i.e., area(13, 11) with two parameters.

Example:

```
// Program to illustrate
// the use of function
package main
import "fmt"
// area() is used to find
```

```
// area of rectangle
// area() function two parameters,
// i.e, length and width
func area(length, width int)int{
    arr := length* width
    return arr
}
// the main function
func main() {
    // Display area of the rectangle
    // with the method calling
    fmt.Printf("Area of rectangle is : %d",
area(13, 11))
}
```

Function Arguments

The arguments provided to a function are referred to as actual parameters in Go, meanwhile the parameters received by a function are referred to as formal parameters.

Note: The Go language uses the call by value technique by default to pass parameters in a function.

The Go programming language provides the following two methods for passing parameters to our function.

Call by Value

In this way of parameter passing, the values of actual parameters are transferred to the function's formal parameters, and two types of parameters are kept in distinct memory locations. As a result, any changes performed within functions are not reflected in the caller's real arguments.

Example:

```
// Program to illustrate
// the concept of call by value
package main
import "fmt"
// function which swap the values
func swap(x, y int)int{
    var o int
    o= x
    x=y
```

```
    y=o
    return o
}
// the main function
func main() {
 var a int = 20
 var b int = 30
  fmt.Printf("a = %d and b = %d", a, b)
 // call by values
 swap(a, b)
    fmt.Printf("\n a = %d and b = %d",a, b)
}
```

Call by Reference

Because both the actual and formal parameters refer to identical locations, any changes performed within the function are reflected in the caller's actual parameters.

Example:

```
// Program to illustrate
// the concept of call by reference
package main
import "fmt"
// function which swap the values
func swap(x, y *int)int{
    var o int
    o = *x
    *x = *y
    *y = o
    return o
}
// the main function
func main() {
var a int = 20
 var b int = 10
  fmt.Printf("a = %d and b = %d", a, b)
// call by reference
  swap(&a, &b)
    fmt.Printf("\n a = %d and b = %d", a, b)
}
```

FUNCTION RETURNING MULTIPLE VALUES

The return statement in the Go programming language allows us to return numerous values from a function. In other words, a single return statement in a function might return many values. The return values are of the same type as the parameters given in the parameter list.

Syntax:

```
func functionname(parameterlist)(returntypelist){
    // code...
}
```

Example:

```
// Program to illustrate how a
// function return the multiple values
package main
import "fmt"
// myfunc return 3 values of int type
func myfunc(x, y int)(int, int, int ){
    return x - y, x * y, x + y
}
// the main Method
func main() {
    // return values are assigned into different
variables
    var myvar1, myvar2, myvar3 = myfunc(4, 2)
    // Display-values
    fmt.Printf("The Result is: %d", myvar1 )
    fmt.Printf("\nThe Result is: %d", myvar2)
    fmt.Printf("\nThe Result is: %d", myvar3)
}
```

Giving Names to the Return Values

Return values in the Go programming language can be given names. We can use such variable names in our code as well. It is not required to include a return statement with these identifiers since the Go compiler will recognize that these variables must send back. The bare return is the name given to this form of return. The use of a bare return minimizes redundancy in our program.

Syntax:

```
func functionname(para1, para2 int)(name1 int,
name2 int){
    // code
}
```

Name1 and name2 are names of the return values, while para1 and para2 are the function arguments.

Example:

```
// illustrate how to give names to return values
package main
import "fmt"
// myfunc return 2 values of the int type
// here, return value name
// is rectangle & square
func myfunc(x, y int)( rectangle int, square int )
{
    rectangle = x*y
    square = x*x
    return
}
func main() {
    // The return values are assigned into the two
different variables
    var area1, area2 = myfunc(4, 8)
    // Display the values
    fmt.Printf("Area of the rectangle is: %d",
area1 )
    fmt.Printf("\nThe Area of the square is: %d",
area2)

}
```

VARIADIC FUNCTIONS

A variadic function is one that is called with a variable number of parameters. In other words, the variadic function accepts zero or more inputs from the user. fmt. Printf is an example of variadic function; it requires one fixed argument at the start and may accept any number of arguments after that.

Important Notes:

- The last parameter type in the variadic function's declaration is preceded by an ellipsis, i.e., (...). It denotes that the function can be invoked with any number of this kind of parameters.

Syntax:

```
function function-name(para1, para2...type)type{
// code
}
```

- Within the function...type acts similarly to a slice. Assume we have a function signature, such as add(b...int)int, and the an argument is of type[]int.

- In a variadic function, you may also provide an existing slice. As illustrated in the second example, we send a slice of the entire array to the function to do this.

- When no arguments are passed to the variadic function, the slice within the function is nil.

- Variadic functions are commonly used to format strings.

- In the variadic method, you may also pass several slices.

- Variadic parameters cannot be used as return values, although they can be returned as slices.

First example:

```
// Program to illustrate
// the concept of variadic function
package main
import(
    "fmt"
    "strings"
)
// Variadic function to join the strings
func joinstr(element...string)string{
    return strings.Join(element, "-")
}
func main() {
```

```
    // zero argument
    fmt.Println(joinstr())
    // the multiple arguments
    fmt.Println(joinstr("Hello", "HEW"))
    fmt.Println(joinstr("Hello", "Everyone",
"World"))
    fmt.Println(joinstr("H", "E", "L", "L", "O"))
}
```

Second example:

```
// Program to illustrate
// the concept of variadic function
package main
  import(
     "fmt"
     "strings"
)
// The Variadic function to join strings
func joinstr(element...string)string{
    return strings.Join(element, "-")
}
func main() {
    // pass a slice in the variadic function
    element:= []string{"hello", "FROM", "world"}
    fmt.Println(joinstr(element...))
}
```

When we utilize a variadic function:

- A variadic function is used to pass a slice in a function.

- We utilize a variable function when we don't know the number of parameters.

- When we utilize a variadic function in your software, it improves readability.

Anonymous Functions

An anonymous function is a feature of the Go programming language. An anonymous function does not have a name when we need to write an inline function. An anonymous function in Go can construct a closure. Anonymous function is also referred to as function literal.

Syntax:

```
func(parameter-list)(returntype){
// code
// Use the return statement if returntype are
given
// if returntype is not given, then do not
// use the return statement
return
}()
```

Example:

```
// Program to illustrate how
// to create anonymous function
package main
import "fmt"
func main() {
    // the anonymous function
    func(){
        fmt.Println("Welcome to World")
    }()
}
```

Important Notes:

- Anonymous function can assign to a variable in the Go programming language. When we assign a function to a variable, the variable's type changes to function, and we may call it a function call, as illustrated in the following example:

```
// Program to illustrate
// the use of an anonymous function
package main
import "fmt"
func main() {
    // Assigning anonymous
    // function to variable
    value := func(){
        fmt.Println("Welcome to World")
    }
    value()
}
```

- In the anonymous function, we may also pass parameters.

Example:

```
// Program to pass arguments
// in anonymous function
package main
import "fmt"func main() {
    // Passing arguments in the anonymous function
  func(ele string){
      fmt.Println(ele)
  }("Helloeveryone")

}
```

- An anonymous function can also pass as an argument to another function.

Example:

```
// Program to pass an anonymous
// function as an argument into
// the other function
package main
import "fmt"
  // Passing anonymous function
  // as argument
  func XYZ(i func(a, b string)string){
      fmt.Println(i ("Hello", "for"))
  }
func main() {
    value:= func(a, b string) string{
        return a + b + "Hello"
    }
    XYZ(value)
}
```

- Another function can also return an anonymous function.

Example:

```
// Program to illustrate
// the use of anonymous function
```

```
package main
import "fmt"
// Returning the anonymous function
 func XYZ() func(a, b string) string{
     myf := func(a, b string)string{
          return a + b + "Everyone"
     }    return myf
 }func main() {
     value := XYZ()
     fmt.Println(value("Hello ", "to "))
 }
```

GoLang main() and init() Functions

The Go programming language reserves two functions for special purposes: main() and init().

main() Function

The main package in Go is a special package used with executable applications, including the main() method. The main() function is a unique function that serves as the executable program's entry point. It neither accepts nor returns any arguments. Go calls the main() method automatically thus there is no need to call it directly, and every executable program must have a single main package and the main() function.

Example:

```
// Program to illustrate
// the concept of main() function
// Declaration of main package
package main
// Importing packages
import (
    "fmt"
    "sort"
    "strings"
    "time"
)
// Main function
func main() {
    // Sorting the given slice
    st := []int{335, 79, 113, 14, 86, 12, 467, 9}
    sort.Ints(st)
```

```
    fmt.Println("Sorted slice: ", st)
    // Finding the index
    fmt.Println("Index value: ", strings.
Index("Hello", "ks"))
    // Finding the time
    fmt.Println("Time: ", time.Now().Unix())
}
```

init() Function

The init() function, like the main function, takes no arguments and returns nothing. This function is contained in every package and is called when the package is first loaded. This function is defined implicitly, so we cannot access it elsewhere. We may construct many init() functions in the same application, and they will execute in the order in which they are created. init() functions can be placed anywhere in the program and are called in lexical file name order (Alphabetical Order). And it is permissible to include statements if the init() function is used, but keep in mind that the init() method is performed before the main() function call; thus it is not dependent on the main() function.

The init() function's main purpose is to initialize global variables that cannot initialize in the global context.

Example:

```
// Program to illustrate
// the concept of init() function
// Declaration of main package
package main
// the importing package
import "fmt"
// the multiple init() function
func init() {
    fmt.Println("Welcome everyone")
}
func init() {
    fmt.Println("Hello everyone ")
}
// the main function
func main() {
    fmt.Println("Welcome to home")
}
```

In GoLang, What Is a Blank Identifier (Underscore)?

In GoLang, _(underscore) is referred to as the Blank Identifier. Identifiers are the user-defined names of the software components used for identification. GoLang provides a feature that allows us to declare and utilize an unused variable using a Blank Identifier. Unused variables are defined by the user throughout the program but are never utilized by them. These variables make the program nearly illegible. Because GoLang is a more concise and readable programming language, it does not enable the programmer to specify an unneeded variable; if we do, the compiler will give an error.

When a function returns several values, but we only need a few of them and discard some of them, we may use the Blank Identifier. It informs the compiler that this variable isn't needed and may disregard without causing an error. It conceals the values of the variables and makes the program intelligible. As a result, anytime we provide a value to Bank Identifier, it becomes useless.

First example: In the following program, the function mul_div returns two values, which we store in the mul and div identifiers. However, throughout the program, we only use one variable, mul. As a result, the compiler will report an error if a div is declared but not utilized.

```
// Program to show compiler
// throws an error if variable is
// declared but not used
package main
import "fmt"
// the main function
func main() {
    // calling function
    // function returns two values which are
    // assigned to mul and div the identifier
    mul, div := mul_div(110, 9)
    // only using the mul variable
    // compiler will give an error
    fmt.Println("110 x 9 = ", mul)
}
// function returning the two
// values of integer type
func mul_div(nm1 int, nm2 int) (int, int) {
    // returning values
    return nm1 * nm2, nm1 / nm2
}
```

Second example: To fix the above program, let's utilize the Blank Identifier. Simply use the _(underscore) in place of the div identification. It allows the compiler to disregard the declared and not used error for that specific variable.

```go
// Program to the use of Blank identifier
package main
import "fmt"
// the main function
func main() {
    // calling function
    // function returns two values which are
    // assigned to mul and blank identifier
    mul, _ := mul_div(110, 8)
    // only using the mul variable
    fmt.Println("110 x 8 = ", mul)
}
// function returning the two
// values of integer type
func mul_div(nm1 int, nm2 int) (int, int) {
    // returning the values
    return nm1 * nm2, nm1 / nm2
}
```

Important Notes:

- Multiple Blank Identifiers can use in the same program. As a result, a GoLang program might contain numerous variables with the same identifier name, the Blank Identifier.

- There are numerous occasions where values must assign just to complete the syntax, even though the values will never utilize in the program. As in a function that returns many values. In such instances, a blank identification is often used.

- With the Blank Identifier, we may utilize any value of any type.

DEFER KEYWORD

Defer statements in Go language postpone the execution of the function or method or an anonymous method until the nearby functions return. Deferred function or method call parameters, in other words, evaluate immediately but do not execute until the nearby function returns. We may construct a delayed method, function, or anonymous function using the defer keyword.

Syntax:

```
// Function
defer func func-name(parameterlist Type)
returntype{
// Code
}
// Method
defer func (receiver Type)
methodname(parameterlist){
// Code
}
defer func (parameterlist)(returntype){
// code
}()
```

Important Notes:

- Multiple defer statements are permitted in the same program in Go, and they are executed in LIFO (Last-In, First-Out) sequence, as illustrated in the second example.

- The parameters in deferring statements are assessed when the defer statement is performed, not when it is called.

- Defer statements are commonly used to guarantee that files are closed when their use is no longer required, to close the channel, or to capture panics in the program.

Let us illustrate this notion with an example:

First example:

```
// Program to illustrate
// the concept of the defer statement
package main
import "fmt"
// Functions
func mul(x1, x2 int) int {
```

```
        rest := x1 * x2
        fmt.Println("Result: ", rest)
        return 0
}
func show() {
        fmt.Println("Hello, Everyone")
}
// the main function
func main() {
        // Calling the mul() function
        // Here the mul function behaves
        // like normal function
        mul(43, 25)
        // Calling the mul()function
        // Using defer keyword
        // Here mul() function
        // is defer function
        defer mul(27, 46)
        // Calling show() function
        show()
}
```

Explanation: In the preceding example, there are two methods named mul() and show() (). Whereas the show() function is generally called in the main() function, the mul() function is called in two ways:

First, we call the mul function normally (no defer keyword), i.e., mul(43, 25), and it executes when the function is invoked.

Second, we use the defer keyword to refer to the mul() function as a deferred function, i.e., defer mul(27, 46), and it executes when all of the surrounding methods return.

Second example:

```
// Program to illustrate
// the multiple defer statements, to illustrate
LIFO policy
package main
import "fmt"
// Functions
func add(x1, x2 int) int {
        rest := x1 + x2
        fmt.Println("Result: ", rest)
```

```
        return 0
}
// the main function
func main() {
    fmt.Println("Starting")
    // Multiple defer statements
    // Executes in the LIFO order
    defer fmt.Println("Ending")
    defer add(37, 59)
    defer add(12, 12)
}
```

PANIC IN GoLang

Panic, like an exception, occurs during runtime in the Go programming language. In other words, panic occurs when an unexpected circumstance occurs in your Go program, causing the execution of your program to be terminated. Sometimes panic occurs during runtime when a specific condition arises, such as out-of-bounds array accesses, as demonstrated in the first example, and other times it is deliberately thrown by the programmer to handle the worst-case scenario in the Go program using the panic() function, as shown in the second example.

The panic function is an inherent function defined in the Go language's built-in package. This function stops the flow of control and begins panicking.

Syntax:

```
func panic(v interface{})
```

It can accept any kind of argument. When a panic occurs in a Go program, the program stops at runtime, and an error message and the stack trace up to the point where the panic occurred are displayed on the output screen. In general, when a panic occurs in a Go program, the program does not terminate immediately; instead, it ends after Go completes all pending work for that program.

For example, if a function A calls panic, the execution of the function A is halted, and if any delayed functions are available in A, they run normally. After that, the function A returns to its caller, and A behaves like a call to panic to the caller. As seen in third example, this procedure is continued until all of the functions in the current goroutine are returned, at which time the program fails.

First example:

```go
// Program which illustrates the
// concept of panic
package main
import "fmt"
// the main function
func main() {
    // Creating array of string type
    // Using the var keyword
    var myarr [3]string
    // Elements are assigned using an index
    myarr[0] = "HE"
    myarr[1] = "Helloeveryone"
    myarr[2] = "Hello"
    // Accessing elements
    // of the array
    // Using the index value
    fmt.Println("The Elements of Array:")
    fmt.Println("The Element 1: ", myarr[0])
    // Program panics because the
    // size of the array is 3
    // we try to access
    // the index 5 which is not
    // available in current array,
    // it gives an runtime error
    fmt.Println("The Element 2: ", myarr[5])
}
```

Second example:

```go
// Program which illustrates
// how to create own panic
// Using the panic function
package main
import "fmt"
// Function
func entry(lang *string, aname *string) {
    // When value of lang
    // is nil it will panic
    if lang == nil {
        panic("Error: The Language cannot be nil")
    }
```

```
    // When value of aname
    // is nil it will panic
    if aname == nil {
        panic("Error: The Author name cannot be
nil")
    }
    // When values of the lang and aname
    // are non-nil values it will print
    // the normal output
    fmt.Printf("The Author Language: %s \n Author
Name: %s\n", *lang, *aname)
}
// the main function
func main() {
    A_lang := "GO-Language"
    // Here in the entry function, we pass
    // a non-nil, nil values
    // Due to nil value this method panics
    entry(&A_lang, nil)
}
```

Third example:

```
// Program which illustrates
// the concept of Defer while panicking
package main
import (
    "fmt"
)
// Function
func entry(lang *string, aname *string) {

    // the Defer statement
    defer fmt.Println("The Defer statement in the
entry function")
    // When value of lang
    // is nil it will panic
    if lang == nil {
        panic("Error: The Language cannot be nil")
    }
    // When value of aname
    // is nil it will panic
    if aname == nil {
```

```
        panic("Error: The Author name cannot be
nil")
    }
    // When values of the lang and aname
    // are non-nil values it will
    // print the normal output
    fmt.Printf("The Author Language: %s \n Author
Name: %s\n", *lang, *aname)
}
// the main function
func main() {
    A_lang := "GO-Language"
    // the Defer statement
    defer fmt.Println("the Defer statement in the
main function")
    // in entry function, we pass
    // one non-nil and one-nil value
    // Due to nil value this method panics
    entry(&A_lang, nil)
}
```

Note that the Defer statement or function is always executed even if the program panics.

Panic's Usage

- We can use panic to indicate an unrecoverable error in which the program cannot continue running.

- If we want an error for a specific circumstance in our program, we may use panic.

RECOVER

Similar to how try/catch blocks in languages like Java, C#, and others are used to catch exceptions, the recover function in Go is used to handle panic. It is a built-in function defined in the Go language's built-in package. This method is mainly used to regain control of a panicked goroutine. In other words, it deals with the goroutine's panicked behavior.

Syntax:

```
func recover() interface{}
```

Quick Points

- The recover function is always invoked within the delayed function and never in the regular function. Using the recover function from within the normal function or outside the delayed function, the panicking sequence continues, as demonstrated in the first example. As shown in the second example, the recover function is always called inside deferred function because deferred function does not stop its execution if program panics, so the recover function stops the panicking sequence by simply restoring normal execution of the goroutine and retrieving the error value passed to the panic call.

- The recover function will only work if we call it in the same goroutine where the panic occurred. It will not work as demonstrated in the third example if we call it in a separate goroutine.

- If we want to find the stack trace, utilize the PrintStack method from the Debug package.

First example:

```
// Program which illustrates
// the concept of recover
package main

import "fmt"

// This function is created to handle
 panic occurs in entry function
// but it does not handle panic
occurred in entry function
// because it called in normal
 function
func handlepanic() {

    if a := recover(); a != nil {
        fmt.Println("RECOVER", a)
    }
}

// Function
func entry(lang *string, aname *string) {
```

```go
    // Normal function
    handlepanic()

    // When value of lang
    // is nil it will panic
    if lang == nil {
        panic("Error: Language cannot be nil")
    }
    // When value of aname
    // is nil it will panic
    if aname == nil {
        panic("Error: Author name cannot be nil")
    }
    fmt.Printf("The Author Language: %s \n Author
Name: %s\n", *lang, *aname)
    fmt.Printf("Return successfully from entry
function")
}
// The main function
func main() {
    A_lang := "GO Language"
    entry(&A_lang, nil)
    fmt.Printf("Return successfully from the main
function")
}
```

CLOSURE

An anonymous function is a feature of the Go programming language. An anonymous function can form a closure. A closure is a sort of anonymous function that refers to variables specified outside of the function. It is analogous to accessing global variables available before the function's declaration.

Example:

```go
// Program to illustrate how
// to create Closure
package main
import "fmt"
func main() {
```

```go
    // Declaring variable
    HFW := 0
    // Assigning an anonymous
    // function to variable
    counter := func() int {
        HFW += 1
        return HFW
    }
    fmt.Println(counter())
    fmt.Println(counter())
}
```

Explanation: The variable HFW was not passed as an argument to the anonymous function, yet it is accessible to the function. This example has a minor issue since any other function specified in the main has to access the global variable HFW and can update it without invoking the counter function. As a result, closure also provides another benefit: data isolation.

```go
// Program to illustrate how
// to create the data isolation
package main
import "fmt"
// newCounter function to
// isolate the global variable
func newCounter() func() int {
    HFW := 0
    return func() int {
        HFW += 1
        return HFW
    }
}
func main() {
    // newCounter function is assigned to a
variable
    counter := newCounter()
    // invoke the counter
    fmt.Println(counter())
    // invoke the counter
    fmt.Println(counter())
}
```

Explanation: The closure refers to the variable HFW even after the new-Counter() function has been completed, but no other code outside the newCounter() method has access to it. This is how data persistency across function calls is maintained while also isolating the data from other programs.

RECURSION

Recursion is the process through which function calls itself, either implicitly or explicitly, and associated function is known as a recursive function. The anonymous function is a particular feature of the Go programming language. It is a function that does not have a name. It is used in the creation of an inline function. Anonymous recursive functions can also be specified and defined. Recursive anonymous functions are also referred to as recursive function literals.

Syntax:

```
func (parameterlist) (returntype) {
// code
// call the same function
// within function for recursion
// Use the return statement only
// if return-type are given.
return
} ()
```

First example:

```
// Program to show
// how to create recursive
// Anonymous function
package main
import "fmt"
func main() {
    // Anonymous function
    var recursiveAnonymous func()
    recursiveAnonymous = func() {
        // Printing message to show
        // the function call and iteration.
        fmt.Println("The Anonymous functions could
be recursive.")
```

```
                    // Calling the same function
recursively
            recursiveAnonymous()
    }
    // the main calling of function
    recursiveAnonymous()
}
```

Second example:

```
// Program to show
// how to create recursive
// Anonymous function
package main
import (
    "fmt"
)
func main() {
    // the Anonymous function
    var recursiveAnonymous func(int)
    // Passing arguments to Anonymous function
    recursiveAnonymous = func(variable int) {
        // Checking condition to return
        if variable == -1 {
            fmt.Println("Welcome to our Channel")
            return
        } else {
            fmt.Println(variable)
            // Calling the same
            // function recursively
            recursiveAnonymous(variable - 1)
        }
    }
    // the main calling
    // of function
    recursiveAnonymous(10)
}
```

Recursion Types

There are several varieties of recursion, as illustrated by the following examples.

Direct Recursion

A direct recursion is a type of recursion in which the function calls itself directly without the help of another function. The following example shows the concept of direct recursion:

```go
// Program to illustrate
// the concept of direct recursion
package main
import (
    "fmt"
)
// the recursive function for
// calculating factorial of a positive integer
func factorial_calc(number int) int {
    // this is base condition
    // if number is 0 or 1 the function will return 1
    if number == 0 || number == 1 {
        return 1
    }
    // if the negative argument is
    // given, it prints error message & returns -1
    if number < 0 {
        fmt.Println("Invalid-number")
        return -1
    }
    // the recursive call to itself with argument
decremented
    // by 1 integer so that it
    // eventually reaches base case
    return number*factorial_calc(number - 1)
}
// main function
func main() {
    // passing 0 as a parameter
    answer1 := factorial_calc(0)
    fmt.Println(answer1, "\n")
    // passing a positive integer
    answer2 := factorial_calc(5)
    fmt.Println(answer2, "\n")
    // passing negative integer
    // prints error message
    // with return value of -1
    answer3 := factorial_calc(-1)
```

```go
    fmt.Println(answer3, "\n")
    // passing positive integer
    answer4 := factorial_calc(10)
    fmt.Println(answer4, "\n")
}
```

Indirect Recursion

An indirect recursion is a sort of recursion in which a function calls another function, which then calls the calling function. Another function is used to assist with this form of recursion. The function does call itself, but it does so indirectly via another function. The following example illustrates the concept of indirect recursion:

```go
// Program to illustrate
// the concept of indirect recursion
package main
import (
    "fmt"
)
// the recursive function for printing all numbers
// upto number x
func print_one(x int) {
    // if number is positive
    // print the number
    // call second function
    if x >= 0 {
        fmt.Println("In first function:", x)
        // call to the second function
        // which calls this first
        // function indirectly
        print_two(x - 1)
    }
}
  func print_two(x int) {
    // if number is positive
    // print the number, call second function
    if x >= 0 {
        fmt.Println("In second function:", x)
        // call to first function
        print_one(x - 1)
    }
}
```

```go
// main function
func main() {
    // passing positive
    // parameter which prints all
    // the numbers from 1 - 10
    print_one(10)
    // this will not print anything as it does not
    // follow base case
    print_one(-1)
}
```

Note: Mutual recursion refers to an indirect recursion with only two functions. To assist indirect recursion, there might be more than two functions.

Tail Recursion

A tail call is a subroutine call that is the last or last call made by the function. When a tail call calls the same function again, the function is said to be tail-recursive. The recursive call is the final thing the function does in this case.

Example:

```go
// Program to illustrate
// the concept of tail recursion
package main
import (
    "fmt"
)
// the tail recursive function
// to print all the numbers
// from x to 1
func print_num(x int) {
    // if number is still
    // positive, print it
    // and call the function
    // with decremented value
    if x > 0 {
        fmt.Println(x)
        // last statement in
        // the recursive function
```

```
        // tail recursive call
        print_num(x-1)
    }
}
  // the main function
func main() {
    // passing positive
    // number, prints 5 to 1
    print_num(5)
}
```

Head Recursion

The recursive call is the initial statement in the function in a head recursion. There are no further statements or operations preceding the call. The function does not need to process anything when called, and all operations are completed when it returns.

Example:

```
// Program to illustrate
// the concept of head recursion
package main
import (
    "fmt"
)
// the head recursive function
// to print all the numbers
// from 1 to x
func print_num(x int) {
        // if the number is still
    // less than x, call
    // function with decremented value
    if x > 0 {
        // the first statement in function
        print_num(x-1)
        // printing is done at
        // the returning time
        fmt.Println(x)
    }
}
// the main function
func main() {
```

```
        // passing positive
        // number, prints 5 to 1
        print_num(5)
}
```

Note: It is worth noting that the output of head recursion is exactly the opposite of that of tail recursion. This is because, in tail recursion, the function prints the number first and then calls itself, but in head recursion, the function calls itself until it reaches the base case and then begins printing while returning.

Infinite Recursion

All of the recursive functions were definite or finite recursive functions, which means they terminated when they reached a base condition. Infinite recursion is a recursion that never converges to a base case and continues indefinitely. This frequently leads to system crashes or memory spills.

Example:

```
// Program to illustrate
// the concept of infinite recursion
package main
import (
    "fmt"
)
// infinite-recursion function
func print_hello() {
    // printing infinite-times
    fmt.Println("Helloeveryone")
    print_hello()
}
// the main function
func main() {
    // call to infinite recursive-function
    print_hello()
}
```

Anonymous Function Recursion

There is a concept in GoLang known as functions that do not have a name. These are known as anonymous functions. Anonymous functions in GoLang can also be used for recursion, as seen in the following examples.

First example:

```
// Program to illustrate
// the concept of anonymous function recursion
package main
import (
    "fmt"
)
// main function
func main() {
    // declaring anonymous function
    // that takes integer value
        var anon_func func(int)
    // defining the anonymous
    // function that prints the numbers from x to 1
        anon_func = func(number int) {
            // the base case
            if number == 0 {
                    return
            } else {
            fmt.Println(number)
            // calling anonymous function
recursively
                    anon_func(number-1)
            }
        }
    // call to anonymous recursive function
        anon_func(5)
}
```

Second example:

```
// Program which illustrates the
// concept of recover
package main
import (
    "fmt"
)
// This function handles panic
// occur in the entry function
// with help of the recover function
func handlepanic() {
        if x := recover(); x != nil {
```

```go
        fmt.Println("RECOVER", x)
    }
}
// Function
func entry(lang *string, aname *string) {
    // the Deferred function
    defer handlepanic()

    // When value of lang is nil it will panic
    if lang == nil {
        panic("Error: The Language cannot be nil")
    }
    // When value of aname
    // is nil it will panic
    if aname == nil {
        panic("Error: The Author name cannot be
nil")
    }
    fmt.Printf("The Author Language: %s \n Author
Name: %s\n", *lang, *aname)
    fmt.Printf("The Return successfully from entry
function")
}
// the main function
func main() {
    A_lang := "GO-Language"
    entry(&A_lang, nil)
    fmt.Printf("The Return successfully from main
function")
}
```

Third example:

```go
// Program which illustrates
// the recover in a goroutine
package main
import (
    "fmt"
    "time"
)
// For the recovery
func handlepanic() {
    if x := recover(); x != nil {
```

```go
        fmt.Println("RECOVER", x)
    }
}
/* Here, this panic is not handled by recover
   function because of recover function is not
   called in the same goroutine in which
 panic occurs */
// the Function 1
func myfun1() {
    defer handlepanic()
    fmt.Println("Welcome to the Function1")
    go myfun2()
    time.Sleep(10 * time.Second)
}
// the Function 2
func myfun2() {
    fmt.Println("Welcome to Function2")
    panic("Panicked!!")
}
// the main function
func main() {
    myfun1()
    fmt.Println("The Return successfully from main
function")
}
```

We covered Function in this chapter, where we talked about returning multiple values, variadic functions, and closure. We also spoke about recursion, defer, panic, and recovery.

CHAPTER 8

Pointers

IN THIS CHAPTER

➤ The * and & operators

➤ New

In Chapter 7, we covered Functions, Closure, and Recursion. We also discussed Defer, Panic, and Recover. In this chapter, we will discuss * and & pointers.

GoLang POINTERS

Pointers are variables in the Go programming language, or GoLang used to hold the memory address of another variable. Pointers are also known as special variables in GoLang. The variables are used to store data in the system at a specific memory address. Memory addresses are always in hexadecimal format (starting with 0x like 0xFFAAF etc.).

What Is the Purpose of a Pointer?

To understand this need, we must first grasp the idea of variables. Variables are the names assigned to memory locations where actual data is stored. To retrieve the stored data, we need to know the address of that specific memory location. Manually remembering all of the memory locations (Hexadecimal Format) is an overhead, which is why we utilize variables to store data, and variables may retrieve simply by using their name.

DOI: 10.1201/9781003310457-8

GoLang also allows us to save a hexadecimal number into a variable using the literal expression, which means that any number beginning with 0x is a hexadecimal number.

Example: In the following program, we save the hexadecimal number in a variable. However, we can see that the value type is int, and it is saved as a decimal value, or we may say that the decimal value of type int is storing. But the essential point of this example is that we are storing a hexadecimal value, but it is not a pointer because it is not referring to another variable's memory location. It is simply a variable that the user has specified. As a result, pointers are required.

```
// Program to demonstrate the variables
// storing hexadecimal values
package main
import "fmt"
func main() {
    // storing hexadecimal
    // values in the variables
    c := 0xFF
    d := 0x9C
    // Displaying values
    fmt.Printf("The Type of variable x is %T\n", c)
    fmt.Printf("The Value of x in hexadecimal is
%X\n", c)
    fmt.Printf("The Value of x in decimal is
%v\n", c)
    fmt.Printf("The Type of variable y is %T\n", d)
    fmt.Printf("The Value of y in hexadecimal is
%X\n", d)
    fmt.Printf("The Value of y in decimal is
%v\n", d)
}
```

A pointer is a kind of variable that contains the memory addresses of other variables and points where the memory is located and gives methods for determining the value stored at that memory location. It is sometimes referred to as a Special Type of Variable since it is virtually exactly specified as a variable but with * (dereferencing operator).

Declaration and Initialization of Pointers

Before we begin, two key operators will use in pointers, namely:

- The '*' dereferencing operator, commonly known as the pointer variable operator, is used to define a pointer variable and access the value contained in the address.

- The & operator, also known as the address operator, is used to return a variable's address or retrieve a variable's address through a pointer.

Declaring a Pointer

```
var pointername *Data_Type
```

As an example, consider the following string pointer, which can only contain the memory addresses of string variables.

```
var st *string
```

Pointer Initialization

To do this, use the address operator to initialize a pointer with the memory address of another variable, as shown in the following example:

```
// the normal variable declaration
var x = 45
// Initialization of pointer st with
// the memory address of variable x
var st *int = &x
```

Example:

```
// program to demonstrate declaration and
// initialization of pointers
package main
import "fmt"
func main() {
    // taking normal variable
    var a int = 4798
    // the declaration of pointer
    var b *int
    // the initialization of pointer
```

```
    b = &a

        // displaying result
    fmt.Println("The Value stored in a = ", a)
    fmt.Println("The Address of a = ", &a)
    fmt.Println("The Value stored in variable b =
", b)
}
```

Important Considerations

1. A pointer's default or zero-value is always nil. Alternatively, an unini-tialized pointer will always have a nil value.

   Example:

   ```
   // Program to demonstrate the
   // nil value of the pointer
   package main
   import "fmt"
   func main() {
           // taking pointer
       var st *int
           // displaying result
       fmt.Println("st = ", st)
   }
   ```

2. The pointers' declaration and initialization can be done in a single line.

   Example:

   ```
   var st *int = &x
   ```

3. If we mention the data type in addition to the pointer declaration, the pointer will be able to handle the memory location of the specified data type variable. For example, if we take a pointer of string type, the address of the variable we give to a pointer will only be of string data type variable, not any other kind.

4. To avoid the issue above, we can use the var keyword's Type Inference idea. The data type does not need to be specified during

the declaration. The compiler may determine the type of a pointer variable in the same way that the type of a regular variable can. We will not utilize the * operator in this case. It will be determined internally by the compiler as we initialize the variable using the address of another variable.

Example:

```
// Program to demonstrate the
// use of type inference in
// the pointer variables
package main
import "fmt"
func main() {
    // using the var keyword
  • // we are not defining any type with the
variable
    var x = 328
    // taking pointer variable using
    // the var keyword without specifying the type
    var a = &x
    fmt.Println("The Value stored in x = ", x)
    fmt.Println("The Address of x = ", &x)
    fmt.Println("The Value stored in pointer
variable a = ", a)
}
```

5. We may alternatively define and initialize the pointer variables using the shorthand (:=) syntax. If we pass the variable's address to it using the &(address) operator, the compiler will internally determine a pointer variable.

Example:

```
// program to demonstrate the
// use of shorthand syntax in Pointer variables
package main
import "fmt"
func main() {
    // using the := operator to declare and
    // initialize the variable
    x := 328
```

```
        // taking pointer variable using
        // := by assigning it with
        // the address of variable y
        a := &x
        fmt.Println("The Value stored in x = ", x)
        fmt.Println("The Address of x = ", &x)
        fmt.Println("The Value stored in pointer
variable a = ", a)
    }
```

Dereferencing Pointer

The * operator is also known as the dereferencing operator. It is used not only to specify the pointer variable, but also to access the value of a variable to which the pointer points, a process known as indirecting or dereferencing. The value at the location is sometimes referred to as the * operator. Let's look at an example to help us comprehend this concept:

```
// Program to illustrate
// the concept of dereferencing a pointer
package main
import "fmt"
func main() {
    // using the var keyword
    // we are not defining any type with the variable
    var x = 328
    // taking pointer variable using
    // the var keyword without specifying the type
    var a = &x
    fmt.Println("The Value stored in x = ", x)
    fmt.Println("The Address of x = ", &x)
    fmt.Println("The Value stored in pointer variable
a = ", a)
    // this is dereferencing a pointer
    // using * operator before the pointer
    // variable to access value stored at the variable
at which it is pointing
    fmt.Println("The Value stored in y(*a) = ", *a)
}
```

Instead of assigning new value to the variable, we can alter the value of the pointer or memory location.

Example:

```
// Program to illustrate the above mentioned
concept
package main
import "fmt"
func main() {
    // using the var keyword
    // we are not defining any type with the variable
    var x = 458
    // taking pointer variable using
    // the var keyword without specifying the type
    var a = &x
    fmt.Println("The Value stored in y before
changing = ", x)
    fmt.Println("The Address of x = ", &x)
    fmt.Println("The Value stored in pointer
variable a = ", a)
    // this is dereferencing pointer
    // using the * operator before pointer
    // variable to access value stored at the
variable at which it is pointing
    fmt.Println("The Value stored in x(*a) Before
Changing = ", *a)
    // changing the value of x by assigning
    // the new value to the pointer
    *a = 500
     fmt.Println("Value stored in x(*a) after
Changing = ",x)
}
```

In GoLang, How Can We Instantiate a Struct Using the New Keyword?

A struct mainly serves as a container for all other data types. We can easily manipulate/access the data allocated to a struct by utilizing a reference to a struct. In GoLang, we may create struct using the new keyword as well as the Pointer Address Operator, as seen in the following example.

Example: In this case, we can see that we are instantiating a struct with the new keyword.

```
// Program to show how to instantiate struct
// using new keyword
```

```go
package main

import "fmt"
type emp struct {
    name    string
    empid   int
    salary  int
}
func main() {
    // emp1 is a pointer to an instance of emp
    // using the new keyword
    emp1 := new(emp)
    emp1.name = "ABC"
    emp1.empid = 2325
    emp1.salary = 37000
    fmt.Println(emp1)
    // emp2 is an instance of emp
    var emp2 = new(emp)
    emp2.name = "XYZ"
    emp2.salary = 40000
    fmt.Println(emp2)
}
```

POINTERS TO A FUNCTION

Pointers are variables in the Go programming language, or GoLang used to hold the memory address of another variable. We may also pass pointers to the function in the same way variables are. There are two ways to accomplish this.

Create a Pointer and Pass It to the Function

We use a function ptf with an integer type pointer parameter in the following program, instructing the function to accept only pointer type arguments. This function essentially modified the value of the variable y. At the start, y has the value 200. However, following the function call, the value changed to 638, as seen in the output.

```go
// Program to create a pointer and
// passing it to the function
package main
import "fmt"
// taking function with integer
```

```
// the type pointer as an parameter
func ptf(b *int) {
    // dereferencing
    *b = 638
}
 // the main function
func main() {
    // taking normal variable
    var y = 200
        fmt.Printf("Value of y before function call
is: %d\n", y)
    // taking pointer variable and
    // assigning the address
    // of y to it
    var pb *int = &y
    // calling tfunction by
    // passing the pointer to function
    ptf(pb)

    fmt.Printf("Value of y after function call is:
%d\n", y)
}
```

Passing an Address of the Variable to Function Call

In the following program, we do not create a pointer to hold the address of the variable y, as we did in the previous program. We are directly passing the address of y to the function call, which works in the same way as the previously stated manner.

```
// Program to create a pointer and
// passing address of the variable to the function
package main
import "fmt"
// taking function with integer
// the type pointer as an parameter
func ptf(b *int) {
    // dereferencing
    *b = 638
}
// the main function
func main() {
```

```
    // taking normal variable
    var y = 200
    fmt.Printf("Value of y before function call is:
%d\n", y)
    // calling the function by
    // passing address of
    // the variable y
    ptf(&y)
    fmt.Printf("Value of y after function call is:
%d\n", y)
}
```

Note: The variables and pointers in the preceding programs can also be declared using the short declaration operator(:=).

POINTER TO A STRUCT

A pointer is variable that stores memory address of another variable. Pointers are also known as special variables in GoLang. The variables are used to store data in the system at a specific memory address.

A pointer to a struct can also use. In GoLang, a struct is a user-defined type that allows us to group/combine elements of possibly diverse kinds into a single type. To utilize a pointer to a struct, use the & operator, also known as the address operator. GoLang allows programmers to use pointers to access the fields of a structure without explicitly dereferencing it.

> **First example:** We will make a structure called Employee that contains two variables. Create an instance of the struct, i.e., emp, in the main function. Following that, we may send the struct's address to the pointer, which represents the pointer to the struct idea. There is no need to explicitly use dereferencing because it will provide the same effect as shown in the following program:

```
// Program to illustrate
// the concept of the Pointer to struct
package main
import "fmt"
// taking structure
type Employee struct {

    // taking the variables
    name   string
```

```
        empid int
}
// the main Function
func main() {
    // creating instance of the Employee struct type
    emp := Employee{"XYZ", 17028}
    // Here, it is the pointer to struct
    pts := &emp
    fmt.Println(pts)
    // accessing struct fields using pointer
    // but here we are not using
    // the dereferencing explicitly
    fmt.Println(pts.name)
    // same as above by explicitly using the
    // dereferencing concept means
    // the result will be the same
    fmt.Println((*pts).name)
}
```

Second example: We may also use the pointer to change the values of structure members or structure literals, as seen in the following program:

```
// Program to illustrate
// the concept of Pointer to struct
package main

import "fmt"
// taking structure
type Employee struct {
    // taking the variables
    name    string
    empid int
}
// the main Function
func main() {
    // creating instance of the
    // Employee struct type
    emp := Employee{"XYZ", 12038}
    // Here, it is the pointer to struct
    pts := &emp
    // displaying values
    fmt.Println(pts)
```

```
    // updating value of name
    pts.name = "ABC"
    fmt.Println(pts)
}
```

POINTER TO POINTER (DOUBLE POINTER) IN Go

Pointers are variables in the Go programming language, or GoLang used to hold the memory address of another variable. Because a pointer is a special variable, it may point to any variable, even another pointer. Essentially, this appears to be a chain of pointers. When we define a pointer to a pointer, the first pointer stores the address of the second pointer. Double Pointers is another name for this concept.

How to Declare a Pointer to a Pointer

Declaring a pointer to a pointer is the same as declaring a pointer in Go. The distinction is that we must put an additional '*' before the pointer's name. This is usually done when we declare the pointer variable using the var keyword and the type. The following examples and illustration will illustrate the concept much better.

First example: In the following program, the pointer pt2 saves the location of the pointer pt1. Dereferencing pt2, i.e., *pt2, returns the address of variable V, or the value of pointer pt1. If we attempt **pt2, you will get the value of the variable V, which is 200.

```
// Program to illustrate
// the concept of the Pointer to Pointer
package main
import "fmt"
// the main Function
func main() {
        // taking variable
        // of the integer type
    var V int = 200
            // taking a pointer
    // of integer type
    var pt1 *int = &V
            // taking pointer to
    // pointer to pt1
    // storing the address
```

```
    // of pt1 into pt2
    var pt2 **int = &pt1
    fmt.Println("Value of Variable V is = ", V)
    fmt.Println("The Address of variable V is = ",
&V)

    fmt.Println("Value of pt1 is = ", pt1)
    fmt.Println("The Address of pt1 is = ", &pt1)
        fmt.Println("Value of pt2 is = ", pt2)
    // Dereferencing pointer to pointer
    fmt.Println("The Value at the address of pt2
is or *pt2 = ", *pt2)
    // double pointer will give the value of
variable V
    fmt.Println("*(The Value at the address of pt2
is) or **pt2 = ", **pt2)
}
```

Second example: Let's make some changes to the preceding program. Assigning a new value to pointers by modifying their values using dereferencing, as seen in the following program:

```
// Program to illustrate
// the concept of Pointer to Pointer
package main
import "fmt"
// the main Function
func main() {
        // taking variable
    // of the integer type
    var v int = 200
    // taking pointer
    // of the integer type
    var pt1 *int = &v
    // taking pointer to
    // the pointer to pt1
    // storing address
    // of pt1 into pt2
    var pt2 **int = &pt1
    fmt.Println("Value of Variable v is = ", v)
    // changing value of v by assigning
    // new value to the pointer pt1
```

```
    *pt1 = 400
    fmt.Println("The Value stored in v after
changing pt1 = ", v)
    // changing value of v by assigning
    // the new value to the pointer pt2
    **pt2 = 600
    fmt.Println("The Value stored in v after
changing pt2 = ", v)
}
```

COMPARING POINTERS

Pointers are variables in the Go programming language, or GoLang used to hold the memory address of another variable. Pointers are also known as special variables in GoLang. The variables are used to store data in the system at a specific memory address. Memory addresses are always in hexadecimal format (starting with 0x like 0xFFAAF etc.).

In the Go programming language, we may compare two pointers. Two pointer values are only identical if they point to the same memory location or if they are nil. We may compare pointers using the == and != operators given by the Go programming language:

1. **== operator:** Returns true if both pointers point to the same variable. Alternatively, if both pointers refer to different variables, return false.

   Syntax:

   ```
   pointer_1 == pointer_2
   ```

   Example:

   ```
   // program to illustrate
   // the concept of comparing two pointers
   package main
   import "fmt"
   func main() {
       val1 := 5325
       val2 := 469
       // Creating, initializing pointers
       var p1 *int
   ```

```
    p1 = &val1
    p2 := &val2
    p3 := &val1
    // Comparing the pointers with each other
    // Using == operator
    res1 := &p1 == &p2
    fmt.Println("Is p1 pointer is equal to the p2
pointer: ", res1)
    res2 := p1 == p2
    fmt.Println("Is p1 pointer is equal to the p2
pointer: ", res2)
    res3 := p1 == p3
    fmt.Println("Is p1 pointer is equal to the p3
pointer: ", res3)
    res4 := p2 == p3
    fmt.Println("Is p2 pointer is equal to the p3
pointer: ", res4)
    res5 := &p3 == &p1
    fmt.Println("Is p3 pointer is equal to the p1
pointer: ", res5)
}
```

2. **!= operator:** If both pointers refer to the same variable, this operator returns false. Instead, if both pointers refer to separate variables, return true.

Syntax:

```
pointer_1 != pointer_2
```

Example:

```
// Program to illustrate
// the concept of comparing two pointers
package main
import "fmt"
func main() {
    val1 := 22459
    val2 := 467
    // Creating, initializing pointers
    var p1 *int
    p1 = &val1
```

```go
    p2 := &val2
    p3 := &val1
    // Comparing the pointers with each other
    // Using the != operator
    res1 := &p1 != &p2
    fmt.Println("Is p1 pointer not equal to the p2
pointer: ", res1)

    res2 := p1 != p2
    fmt.Println("Is p1 pointer not equal to the p2
pointer: ", res2)
    res3 := p1 != p3
    fmt.Println("Is p1 pointer not equal to the p3
pointer: ", res3)
    res4 := p2 != p3
    fmt.Println("Is p2 pointer not equal to the p3
pointer: ", res4)
    res5 := &p3 != &p1
    fmt.Println("Is p3 pointer not equal to the p1
pointer: ", res5)
}
```

This chapter covered * and & operators and new operator in pointers.

CHAPTER 9

Structs and Interfaces

IN THIS CHAPTER

➢ Structs

➢ Methods

➢ Interfaces

In Chapter 8, we covered pointers, and in this chapter, we will discuss structs, methods, and interfaces.

GoLang STRUCTURES

In GoLang, a structure or struct is a user-defined type that allows us to group/combine elements of possibly diverse kinds into a single type. A struct can represent any real-world thing with a collection of properties/ fields. In general, this idea is related to classes in object-oriented programming. It is a lightweight class that does not support inheritance but supports composition.

An address, for example, includes a name, street, city, state, and Pin code. As seen below, it makes logical to combine all three characteristics into a single structure address.

Declaring a structure:

```
type Address struct {
        name string
        streetno string
        city string
```

DOI: 10.1201/9781003310457-9

187

```
        state string
        Pin-code int
}
```

The type keyword adds a new type in the preceding code. It is followed by the type name (Address) and the keyword struct, indicating that we define a struct. Within the curly braces, the struct has a list of several fields. Each field has a name as well as a kind.

Nota bene: We may also make them more compact by combining many fields of the same kind, as demonstrated in the following example:

```
type Address struct {
    name, streetno, city, state string
    Pin-code int
}
```

To define a structure:

The syntax for declaring a structure is stated below:

```
var x Address
```

The above code creates a variable of type Address, which is initially initialized to zero. Zero indicates that all fields have been set to their corresponding zero value for a struct. So, the fields name, street no., city, and state are all set to "" and the field Pin-code is set to 0.

We may also use a struct literal to initialize a variable of a struct type, as illustrated below:

```
var x = Address{"Abishek", "PritamNagar", "Delhi",
"Noida", 293616}
```

Note:

- Remember to pass the field values in the same order specified in the struct. Furthermore, it is difficult to use the approach above to initialize only a subset of fields.

- Go also provides the name: value syntax (the order of fields is irrelevant when using this syntax). As a result, we can only initialize a subset of the fields. All uninitialized fields are set to their default value of zero.

Example:

```
var x = Address{Name:"Abhishek",
streetno:"PritamNagar", state:"Delhi", Pin-code:
293616} //city:""

// Program to show how to
// declare and define struct
package main
import "fmt"
// Defining struct type
type Address struct {
    Name      string
    city      string
    Pin-code int
}
func main() {
    // Declaring variable of a 'struct' type
    // All the struct fields are initialized with
their zero value
    var x Address
    fmt.Println(x)
    // Declaring and initializing a
    // struct using struct literal
    x1 := Address{"Anisha", "Delhi", 3663272}
    fmt.Println("Address1: ", x1)
    // Naming fields while
    // initializing a struct
    x2 := Address{Name: "Abhishek", city: "Balli",
                                Pincode: 287011}
    fmt.Println("Address2: ", x2)
    // Uninitialized fields are set to
    // their corresponding zerovalue
    x3 := Address{Name: "Amritsar"}
    fmt.Println("Address3: ", x3)
}
```

How Can We Get to Struct Fields?

We must use the dot (.) operator to access specific fields of a struct.

Example:

```
// program to show how to
// access fields of struct
```

```go
package main
import "fmt"
  // defining struct
type Car struct {
    Name, Modelno, Color string
    WeightinKg           float64
}
// the main Function
func main() {
    x := Car{Name: "BMW", Modelno: "BTC2",
            Color: "Black", WeightinKg: 1720}
    // Accessing the struct fields
    // using dot operator
    fmt.Println("Car Name: ", x.Name)
    fmt.Println("Car Color: ", x.Color)
    // Assigning a new value
    // to a struct field
    x.Color = "White"
    // Displaying result
    fmt.Println("Car: ", x)
}
```

Pointers to a Struct

Pointers are variables in the Go programming language, or GoLang used to hold the memory address of another variable. As seen in the following example, we can also build a reference to a struct:

```go
// Program to illustrate
// pointer to the struct
package main
import "fmt"
// defining structure
type Employee struct {
    first-name, last-name string
    age, salary int
}
func main() {
    // passing address of the struct variable
    // empy is a pointer to the Employee struct
    empy := &Employee{"Samrit", "Anders", 35, 7000}
    // (*empy).first-name is the syntax to access
    // the first-name field of the empy struct
```

```
    fmt.Println("First Name:", (*empy).first-name)
    fmt.Println("Age:", (*empy).age)
}
```

We may use empy.first-name instead of the explicit dereference (*empy) in GoLang. To access the first-name field, type first-name. The following is an example to demonstrate this:

```
// Program to illustrate the
// pointer to the struct
package main

import "fmt"
// Defining structure
type Employee struct {
    first-name, last-name string
    age, salary     int
}
// the main Function
func main() {
    // taking pointer to the struct
    empy := &Employee{"Samrit", "Anders", 59, 7000}
    // empy.first-name is used to access
    // the field first-name
    fmt.Println("First Name: ", empy.first-name)
    fmt.Println("Age: ", empy.age)
}
```

GoLang's NESTED STRUCTURE

A structure, also known as a struct in GoLang, is a user-defined type that allows us to group items of multiple kinds into a single unit. A struct can represent any real-world thing with various attributes or fields. The Go programming language supports nested structures. A nested structure is a structure that is the field of another structure. A nested structure is a structure that is enclosed within another structure.

Syntax:

```
type structname1 struct{
  // Fields
}
```

```go
type structname2 struct{
  variablename  structname1
}
```

Let's look at a few instances to assist us to understand this concept:

First example:

```go
// Program to illustrate the
// nested structure
package main
import "fmt"
// Creating the structure
type Author struct {
    name     string
    branchno   string
    year    int
}
// Creating the nested structure
type HR struct {
    // structure as field
    details Author
}
func main() {
    // Initializing fields
    // of the structure
    results := HR{
        details: Author{"Sonali", "EDE", 2014},
    }
    // Display values
    fmt.Println("\nDetails of the Author")
    fmt.Println(results)
}
```

Second example:

```go
// Program to illustrate the
// nested structure
package main
import "fmt"
// Creating the structure
type Students struct {
```

```go
    name     string
    branchno string
    year     int
}
// Creating the nested structure
type Teachers struct {
    name    string
    subject string
    expr    int
    details Students
}
func main() {
    // Initializing fields
    // of the structure
    results := Teachers{
        name:    "Sunita",
        subject: "PHP",
        expr:    2,
        details: Student{"Rahil", "CDE", 4},
    }
    // Display the values
    fmt.Println("Details of the Teachers")
    fmt.Println("Teacher's name: ", results.name)
    fmt.Println("Subject: ", results.subject)
    fmt.Println("Experience: ", results.exp)
    fmt.Println("\nDetails of Students")
    fmt.Println("Student's name: ", results.
details.name)
    fmt.Println("Student's branch name: ",
results.details.branch)
    fmt.Println("Year: ", results.details.year)
}
```

GoLang's ANONYMOUS STRUCTURE AND FIELD

A structure, also known as a struct in GoLang, is a user-defined type that allows us to organize items of multiple kinds into a single unit. A struct can represent any real-world thing with a collection of attributes or fields.

Anonymous Structure

In the Go programming language, we may build an anonymous structure. An anonymous building does not have a name. It is useful to create a structure that will only use once. Use the following syntax to create an anonymous structure:

```
variablename := struct{
// fields
}{// Fieldvalues}
```

Let us illustrate this notion with an example:

```
// Program to illustrate
// the concept of anonymous structure
package main
import "fmt"
// the main function
func main() {
    // Creating, initializing
    // anonymous structure
    Elements := struct {
        name        string
        branch      string
        language    string
        Particles   int
    }{
        name:       "Pihu",
        branch:     "ECE",
        language:   "C#",
        Particles: 298,
    }
    // Display anonymous structure
    fmt.Println(Element)
}
```

Anonymous Fields

We may build anonymous fields in a Go structure. Anonymous fields do not have a name; instead, we specify the field type, and Go will use the type as the field's name. The structure's anonymous fields may be created using the following syntax:

```
type structname struct{
    int
    bool
    float64
}
```

Important Notes:

- It is not permitted to create two or more fields of the same type in a structure, as seen below:

```
type students struct{
int
int
}
```

If we attempt to do so, the compiler will generate an error.

- It is permissible to combine anonymous and named fields, as demonstrated below:

```
type students struct{
 name int
 prices int
 string
}
```

Below is an example to explain the anonymous field concept:

```
// Program to illustrate
// the concept of anonymous structure
package main
import "fmt"
// Creating structure
// with the anonymous fields
type students struct {
    int
    string
    float64
}
// the main function
func main() {
    // Assigning the values to anonymous
    // fields of the students structure
    value := students{143, "Sud", 8200.21}
    // Display values of the fields
    fmt.Println("Enrollment number : ", value.int)
    fmt.Println("Student name : ", value.string)
    fmt.Println("Package price : ", value.float64)
}
```

GoLang METHODS

Methods for Go language support Go methods are identical to Go functions with one exception: the method includes a receiver parameter. The method can access the receiver's properties with the aid of the receiver argument. The receiver can be of either struct or non-struct type in this case. When we write code, the receiver and receiver type must be in the same package. Furthermore, we are not permitted to write a method whose receiver type is already specified in another package, including inbuilt types such as int, string, and so on. If we attempt to do so, the compiler will generate an error.

Syntax:

```
func(reciver-name Type) method-name(parameter-
list)(return-type){
// Code
}
```

Within the method, the receiver may access.

Method with the Struct Type Receiver

We may construct a method whose receiver is of the struct type in the Go programming language. This receiver is available within the method, as seen in the following example:

```
// Program to illustrate
// the method with struct type receiver
package main
import "fmt"
// the author structure
type author struct {
    name        string
    branch      string
    particles   int
    salary      int
}
// Method with a receiver of author type
func (x author) show() {
    fmt.Println("Author's Name: ", x.name)
    fmt.Println("Branch Name: ", x.branch)
    fmt.Println("Published articles: ", x.particles)
```

```go
        fmt.Println("Salary: ", x.salary)
}
// the main function
func main() {
    // Initializing values
    // of the author structure
    rest := author{
        name:      "Monika",
        branch:    "CDE",
        particles: 204,
        salary:    37000,
    }
    // Calling method
    rest.show()
}
```

Method with the Non-Struct Type Receiver

In Go, we may define a method with a non-struct type receiver as long as the type and method declarations are in the same package. If they are present in many packages, such as int, string, and so on, the compiler will generate an error because they are defined in multiple packages.

Example:

```go
// Program to illustrate method
// with the non-struct type receiver
package main
import "fmt"
// Type definition
type data int
// Defining method with
// the non-struct type receiver
func (c1 data) multiply(c2 data) data {
    return c1 * c2
}
/*
// if you try to run this code,
// then compiler will throw an error
func(c1 int)multiply(c2 int)int{
return c1 * c2
}
```

```
*/
// Main function
func main() {
    value1 := data(43)
    value2 := data(26)
    rest := value1.multiply(value2)
    fmt.Println("Final result: ", rest)
}
```

Methods with the Pointer Receiver

A method with a pointer recipient is permitted in the Go programming language. If a modification is made to the method using a pointer receiver, it will be reflected in the caller, which is not feasible with value receiver methods.

Syntax:

```
func (p *Type) method-name(...Type) Type {
// Code
}
```

Example:

```
// Program to illustrate pointer receiver
package main
import "fmt"
// the author structure
type author struct {
    name        string
    branch      string
    particles int
}
// Method with a receiver of the author type
func (x *author) show(abranch string) {
    (*x).branch = abranch
}
// the main function
func main() {
    // Initializing values
    // of the author structure
    rest := author{
```

```
        name:     "Shona",
        branch: "CDE",
    }
    fmt.Println("Author's name: ", rest.name)
    fmt.Println("Branch Name(Before): ", rest.
branch)
    // Creating pointer
    p := &rest
    // Calling show method
    p.show("ERE")
    fmt.Println("Author's name: ", rest.name)
    fmt.Println("Branch Name(After): ", rest.
branch)
}
```

Method Can Accept Both the Pointer and the Value

As we all know, when a function has a value argument, it will only take the values of the parameter, and if we try to give a pointer to a value function, it will reject it, and vice versa. On the other hand, a Go method can accept both a value and a pointer, depending on whether it is specified with a pointer or a value receiver. As illustrated in the following example:

```
// Program to illustrate how
// the method can accept pointer and value
package main
 import "fmt"
// Author structure
type author struct {
    name    string
    branch string
}
// Method with pointer
// receiver of author type
func (x *author) show_1(abranch string) {
    (*x).branch = abranch
}
 // Method with a value
// receiver of author type
func (x author) show_2() {
    x.name = "Gautam"
```

```
        fmt.Println("Author's name(Before)  : ", x.name)
}
// the main function
func main() {

        // Initializing values
        // of the author structure
        rest := author{
            name:    "Sonika",
            branch: "CSA",
        }
        fmt.Println("Branch Name(Before): ", rest.
branch)
        // Calling show_1 method
        // (pointer method) with the value
        res.show_1("ECE")
        fmt.Println("Branch Name(After): ", rest.
branch)
        // Calling show_2 method
        // (value method) with a pointer
        (&rest).show_2()
        fmt.Println("Author's name(After): ", res.namet)
}
```

Difference between the Method and the Function

Method	Function
It includes a receiver.	It does not include a receiver.
In the program, methods with the same name but various kinds might define.	The program does not define functions with the same name but distinct types.
It cannot use to create a first-order object.	It may be used as a first-order object and can be passed.

INTERFACES

The interfaces of the Go language differ from those of other languages. The interface is a special type in Go used to express a set of one or more method signatures. The interface is abstract, thus we cannot make an instance of it. However, we are permitted to establish an interface type variable that may be assigned with a concrete type value that has the methods required by the interface. In other words, the interface is both a set of methods and a custom type.

How Do We Make an Interface?

In the Go programming language, we can define an interface with the following syntax:

```
type interfacename interface{
// Method-signatures
}
```

Example:

```
// Creating interface
type myinterface interface{

// Methods
func1() int
func2() float64
}
```

The interface name is enclosed by the type and interface keywords, while curly brackets enclose the method signatures.

How to Implement Interfaces

In order to implement an interface in the Go language, all of the methods specified in the interface must implement. The interfaces for the Go programming language are implemented implicitly. And, unlike other languages, it lacks a specific term for implementing an interface. As illustrated in the following example.

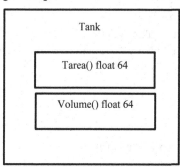

Example:

```
// Program illustrates how
// to implement interface
package main
```

```go
import "fmt"
// Creating interface
type tank interface {
    // Methods
    Tarea() float64
    Volume() float64
}
type myvalue struct {
    radius float64
    height float64
}
// Implementing methods of t
ank interface
func (m myvalue) Tarea() float64
{
        return 2*m.radius*m.height +
           2*3.14*m.radius*m.radius
}
func (m myvalue) Volume() float64
{
    return 3.14 * m.radius * m.radius * m.height
}
// the main Method
func main() {

    // Accessing elements of the
    // tank interface
    var tk tank
    tk = myvalue{10, 14}
    fmt.Println("The Area of tank :", tk.Tarea())
    fmt.Println("The Volume of tank:",
tk.Volume())
}
```

Important Notes:

- The interface's zero value is nil.

- When an interface includes no methods, it is referred to as an empty interface. As a result, all types implement the empty interface.

    Syntax:

    ```go
    interface{}
    ```

- **Interface Types:** There are two types of interfaces: static interfaces and dynamic interfaces. The static type is the interface itself, such as tank in the example below. However, because the interface lacks a static value, it always points to the dynamic values.

  A variable of the interface type contains the value of the type that implements the interface; hence, the value of that type is known as dynamic value, and the type is the dynamic type. It's also referred to as concrete value and concrete type.

Example:

```
// Program to illustrate concept
// of the dynamic values and types
package mainimport "fmt"
// Creating interface
type tank interface {

    // Methods
    Tarea() float64
    Volume() float64
}
func main() {
    var tk tank
    fmt.Println("The Value of the tank interface
is: ", tk)
    fmt.Printf("The Type of the tank interface is:
%T ", tk)
}
```

In the example, we have an interface called a tank. In this example, fmt.Println("The Value of the tank interface is: ", tk) returns the interface's dynamic value, whereas fmt.Printf("The Type of the tank interface is: percent T ", tk) returns the dynamic type, which is nil because the interface does not know who is implementing it.

- **Type Assertions:** A type assertion in Go is an operation performed on the value of an interface. In other words, type assertion is a procedure for extracting the interface's values.

Syntax:

```
a.(T)
```

In this case, a is the interface's value or expression, and T is the type, sometimes known as the asserted type. The type assertion is used to determine whether or not the dynamic type of its operand matches the claimed type. If the T is of concrete type, the type assertion verifies that the specified dynamic type of a is equal to the T; if the verification is successful, the type assertion returns the dynamic value of a. If the checking fails, the operation will fail. If T is an interface type, the type assertion tests if the supplied dynamic type of a satisfies T; if the checking succeeds, the dynamic value is not extracted.

Example:

```
// Program to illustrate the
// type assertion
package main
import "fmt"
func myfun(a interface{}) {
    // Extracting the value of a
    vals := a.(string)
    fmt.Println("Value: ", vals)
}
func main() {
    var val interface {
    } = "Helloeveryone"
    myfun(vals)
}
```

If we alter the val:= a.(string) command in the above example to val:= a.(int), the program panics. To address this issue, we apply the following syntax:

```
value, ok := a.(T)
```

If the type of the a is T, then the value includes the dynamic value of the a, and ok is set to true. And if the type of the a is not equal to T, then ok is set to false, and value contains a value of zero, and the program does not panic. As shown in the following program:

```
// Program to illustrate the type assertion
package main
import "fmt"
func myfun(a interface{}) {
```

```
    value, ok := a.(float64)
    fmt.Println(value, ok)
}
func main() {
    var a1 interface {
    } = 97.09
    myfun(a1)
    var a2 interface {
    } = "Helloeveryone"
    myfun(a2)
}
```

- **Type Switch:** A type switch in a Go interface compares the concrete type of an interface to the numerous types provided in the case statements. It is identical to type assertion with one exception: case specifies types rather than values. A type can also compare to an interface type. As illustrated in the following example:

```
// Program to illustrate the type switch
package main
import "fmt"
func myfun(a interface{}) {
    // Using the type switch
    switch a.(type) {
    case int:
        fmt.Println("Type: int, Value:", a.(int))
    case string:
        fmt.Println("\nType: string, Value: ",
a.(string))
    case float64:
        fmt.Println("\nType: float64, Value: ",
a.(float64))
    default:
        fmt.Println("\nType not found")
    }
}
// the main method
func main() {
    myfun("Helloeveryone")
    myfun(59.9)
    myfun(true)
}
```

- **Use of Interface:** We may use interface when we want to pass multiple sorts of arguments to methods or functions such as the Println () function. When many types implement the same interface, we may also use interface.

Why Go Interfaces Are Great

An "interface" in object-oriented programming describes what an object can accomplish. Typically, this takes the form of a list of methods that an object to have is required. C #, Java supports interfaces, and the Go programming language, although Go's interfaces are notably simple to use.

We don't have to declare that a Go type (which functions similarly to a "class" in other languages) implements an interface, as we would in C# or Java. We just declare the interface, and then any type that has those methods may be used anywhere that interface is required.

Redundant Functions

Assume we have a pet package (a "package" is equivalent to a "library" in other languages) containing Dogs and Cats types. A Dogs has the Fetch technique, a Cats has the Purr method, and both dogs and cats have the Walk and Sit methods.

```
packag pets
import "fmt"
type Dogs struct {
    Name   string
    Breed string
}
func (d Dogs) Walk() {
    fmt.Println(d.Name, "walks across room")
}
func (d Dogs) Sit() {
    fmt.Println(d.Name, "sits down")
}
func (d Dogs) Fetch() {
    fmt.Println(d.Name, "fetches toy")
}
type Cats struct {
    Name   string
    Breed string
}
```

```
func (c Cats) Walk() {
    fmt.Println(c.Name, "walks across room")
}
func (c Cats) Sit() {
    fmt.Println(c.Name, "sits down")
}
func (c Cats) Purr() {
    fmt.Println(c.Name, "purrs")
}
```

Now, let's create an example. Go program that demonstrates what the Dog and Cat types are capable of. We'll create a DemoDog function that takes a Dog and calls the Walk and Sit methods on it. Then, we'll create a DemoCat function that accomplishes the same thing for cats.

```
package main
import "pets"
func DemoDogs(dog pets.Dogs) {
    dog.Walk()
    dog.Sit()
}
func DemoCat(cat pets.Cats) {
    cat.Walk()
    cat.Sit()
}
func main() {
    dog := pets.Dogs{"Fido", "Terrier"}
    cat := pets.Cats{"Fluffy", "Siamese"}
    DemoDogs(dog)
    // call outputs:
    // Fido walks across room
    // Fido sit down
    DemoCat(cat)
    // call outputs:
    // Fluffy walks across room
    // Fluffy sit down
}
```

Unfortunately, the DemoDogs and DemoCats routines are identical, except that one takes a Dogs and the other takes Cats. Because we could alter one function but fail to update the other, repeating code like that increases the risk of inconsistency. It would be perfect if we could get rid of DemoCats and only give Cats to DemoDogs; however, this would lead to an error:

```
DemoDogs(cat)
// ./demo.go:19: cannot use cat (type pets.Cats)
// as type pets.Dogs in argument to DemoDogs
```

Enter Interface

But we don't have to keep two almost identical functions simply because they take different types. This is precisely the problem that interfaces are created to fulfill.

We'll create a FourLegged interface with Walk and Sit methods for all kinds. Then, instead of the DemoDogs and DemoCats functions, we'll replace them with a single Demo function that accepts any FourLegged value (whether it's a Dogs or a Cats).

```
package main
import "pets"
// This interface represents any type that has Walk
and Sit methods.
type FourLegged interface {
    Walk()
    Sit()
}
// We can replace DemoDogs and DemoCats
// with this single function.
func Demo(animal FourLegged) {
    animal.Walk()
    animal.Sit()
}
func main() {
    dog := pets.Dogs{"Rido", "Ferrier"}
    cat := pets.Cats{"Pluffy", "Diames"}
    Demo(dog)
    // Above call (again) outputs:
    // Fido walks across room
    // Fido sit down
    Demo(cat)
    // The above call (again) outputs:
    // Fluffy walks across room
    // Fluffy sit down
}
```

EMBEDDING INTERFACES

The interface in Go is a collection of method signatures and a type, which means you may construct a variable of an interface type. Although the Go language does not enable inheritance, the Go interface does. In embedding, an interface can embed other interfaces or their method signatures, with the same results as seen in first and second examples. We may embed an unlimited number of interfaces in a single interface. And when we embed other interfaces in an interface, if we alter the methods of the interfaces, the changes will be reflected in the embedded interface as well, as illustrated in Example 3.

Syntax:

```
type interfacename1 interface {
    Method1()
}

type interfacename2 interface {
    Method2()
}
type finalinterfacename interface {
    interfacename1
    interfacename2
}
```

First example:

```
// Program to illustrate the concept
// of embedding interfaces
package main
import "fmt"
// Interface 1
type AuthorDetail interface {
    details()
}
// Interface 2
type AuthorArticle interface {
    articles()
}
// Interface 3 embedded with the interface 1 and 2
type FinalDetail interface {
    AuthorDetail
```

```go
        AuthorArticle
}

// Structure
type author struct {
    a_name     string
    branch     string
    college    string
    year       int
    salary     int
    particles int
    tarticles int
}

// Implementing the method of
// the interface 1
func (a author) details() {
    fmt.Printf("The Author Name: %s", a.a_name)
    fmt.Printf("\nThe Branch: %s and passing year:
%d",
                                    a.branch, a.year)
    fmt.Printf("\nThe College Name: %s", a.college)
    fmt.Printf("\nThe Salary: %d", a.salary)
    fmt.Printf("\nThe Published articles: %d",
a.particle)
}
// Implementing method of the interface 2
func (a author) articles() {
    pendingarticle := a.tarticle - a.particle
    fmt.Printf("\nPending articles: %d",
pendingarticle)
}
// the main value
func main() {
    // Assigning values to the structure
    values := author{
        a_name:    "Ricky",
        branch:    "Accounts",
        college:   "XYZ",
        year:      2019,
        salary:    40000,
        particle: 107,
        tarticle: 206,
```

```
    }
    // Accessing methods of the interface 1 and 2
    // Using the FinalDetail interface
    var f FinalDetail = values
    f.details()
    f.articles()
}
```

Explanation: As seen in the preceding example, we have three interfaces. Interfaces 1 and 2 are basic interfaces, but interface 3 is an embedded interface containing interfaces 1 and 2. As a result, any changes made in interfaces 1 and 2 will be reflected in interface 3. And interface 3 has access to all of the methods available in interfaces 1 and 2.

Second example:

```
// Program to illustrate concept of embedding
interfaces
package main
import "fmt"
// Interface 1
type AuthorDetail interface {
    details()
}
// Interface 2
type AuthorArticle interface {
    article()
}
// Interface 3 embedded with the interface 1 and
2's methods
type FinalDetail interface {
    detail()
    article()
}
// Structure
type author struct {
    a_name      string
    branch      string
    college     string
    year        int
    salary      int
    particle int
```

```
        tarticle int
}
    // Implementing method of the interface 1
func (a author) details() {
    fmt.Printf("The Author Name: %s", a.a_name)
    fmt.Printf("\nThe Branch: %s and passing year:
%d", a.branch, a.year)
    fmt.Printf("\nThe College Name: %s",
a.college)
    fmt.Printf("\nThe Salary: %d", a.salary)
    fmt.Printf("\nThe Published articles: %d",
a.particle)
}
// Implementing method of the interface 2
func (a author) articles() {
    pendingarticle := a.tarticle - a.particle
    fmt.Printf("\nThe Pending articles: %d",
pendingarticle)
}
// the main value
func main() {
    // Assigning the values to structure
values := author{
        a_name:    "Ricky",
        branch:    "Accounts",
        college:   "XYZ",
        year:      2019,
        salary:    40000,
        particle: 107,
        tarticle: 206,
    }
    // Accessing the methods
    // of the interface 1 and 2
    // Using the FinalDetail interface
    var f FinalDetail = values
    f.detail()
    f.article()
}
```

Explanation: As seen in the preceding example, we have three interfaces. Interfaces 1 and 2 are basic interfaces, whereas interface 3 is an embedded interface containing method signatures for interfaces 1 and 2. As a consequence, any modifications made to interfaces 1 and 2's methods will be reflected in interface 3. And interface 3 has access to all of the methods available in interfaces 1 and 2.

Third example:

```
// Program to illustrate concept of embedding
interfaces
package main
import "fmt"
// Interface 1
type AuthorDetail interface {
    detail()
}
// Interface 2
type AuthorArticle interface {
    article()
    picked()
}
// Interface 3
// Interface 3 embedded with interface 1's method
and interface 2
// And also contain its own method
type FinalDetail interface {
    detail()
    AuthorArticle
    cdeatil()
}
// Structure
type author struct {
    a_name      string
    branch      string
    college     string
    year        int
    salary      int
    particle int
    tarticle int
    cid         int
    post        string
    pick        int
}
// Implementing method of the interface 1
```

```go
func (a author) detail() {
    fmt.Printf("The Author Name: %s", a.a_name)
    fmt.Printf("\nThe Branch: %s and passing year:
%d", a.branch, a.year)
    fmt.Printf("\nThe College Name: %s",
a.college)
    fmt.Printf("\nThe Salary: %d", a.salary)
    fmt.Printf("\nThe Published articles: %d",
a.particle)
}
// Implementing methods of the interface 2
func (a author) article() {

    pendingarticle := a.tarticle - a.particle
    fmt.Printf("\nPending articles: %d",
pendingarticle)
}
func (a author) picked() {
    fmt.Printf("\nThe Total number of picked
articles: %d", a.pick)
}
// Implementing the method of the embedded
interface
func (a author) cdeatil() {
        fmt.Printf("\nAuthor Id: %d", a.cid)
    fmt.Printf("\nPost: %s", a.post)
}
// the main value
func main() {
    // Assigning values to structure
    values := author{
        a_name:    "Ricky",
        branch:    "Accounts",
        college:   "XYZ",
        year:      2019,
        salary:    40000,
        particle: 107,
        tarticle: 206,
        cid:       3097,
        post:      "Content writer",
        pick:      38,
    }
    // Accessing methods
```

```
    // of the interface 1 and 2
    // Using the FinalDetails interface
    var f FinalDetails = values
    f.detail()
    f.article()
    f.picked()
    f.cdeatil()
}
```

Explanation: As seen in the preceding example, we have three interfaces. Interfaces 1 and 2 are basic interfaces, whereas interface 3 is an embedded interface that contains the method signatures of interfaces 1 and 2 and its own method. As an outcome, any modifications made to the methods of interfaces 1 and 2 will be reflected in interface 3. And interface 3 has access to all of the methods in it, including those in interfaces 1, 2, and its own.

INHERITANCE

One of the most fundamental ideas in object-oriented programming is inheritance, which involves inheriting the properties of the superclass into the base class. Because GoLang does not provide classes, inheritance is accomplished through struct embedding. We cannot directly expand structs, but must instead employ a notion known as composition, in which the struct is used to create additional objects. As a result, there is no inheritance concept in GoLang.

In composition, base structs can be embedded in a child struct, and the base struct's methods can be called directly on the child struct, as demonstrated in the following examples.

First example:

```
// Program to illustrate
// the concept of inheritance
package main
import (
    "fmt"
)
// declaring struct
type Comic struct{
    // declaring the struct variable
    Universe string
}
```

```go
// function to return
// universe of comic
func (comic Comic) ComicUniverse() string {
    // returns the comic universe
    return comic.Universe
}
// declaring struct
type Marvel struct{
    // anonymous field,
    // this is composition where the
    // struct is embedded
    Comic
}
// declaring struct
type DC struct{
    // anonymous field
    Comic
}
// the main function
func main() {

    // creating instance
    cs1 := Marvel{
        // child struct can directly access base
struct variables
            Comic{
            Universe: "MCU",
            },
        }
    // child struct can directly access base
struct methods
    // printing base method using child
        fmt.Println("The Universe is:", cs1.
ComicUniverse())
            cs2 := DC{
        Comic{
            Universe : "DC",
        },
    }
    // printing base method using the child
    fmt.Println("The Universe is:", cs2.
ComicUniverse())
}
```

Multiple inheritance occurs when a child struct has access to various attributes, fields, and methods of more than one base struct. As seen by the following code, the child struct embeds all of the base structs:

Second example:

```
// Program to illustrate
// the concept of multiple inheritances
package main

import (
    "fmt"
)
// declaring first base struct
type first struct{
    // declaring the struct variable
    base_one string
}
// declaring the second base struct
type second struct{
    // declaring the struct variable
    base_two string
}
// function to return first struct variable
func (f first) printBase1() string{
    // returns string of first struct
    return f.base_one
}
// function to return second struct variable
func (s second) printBase2() string{
    // returns string of first struct
    return s.base_two
}
// child struct which embeds both base structs
type child struct{
    // anonymous fields, struct embedding
    // of multiple structs
    first
    second
}
// the main function
func main() {
    // declaring instance
```

```
        // of child struct
        cs1 := child{
            // child struct can directly access base
    struct variables
            first{
                base_one: "In base struct 1.",
            },
            second{
                base_two: "\nIn base struct 2.\n",
            },
        }
        // child struct can directly access base
    struct methods
        // printing the base method
        // using the instance of child struct
        fmt.Println(cs1.printBase1())
        fmt.Println(cs1.printBase2())
    }
```

POLYMORPHISM USING INTERFACES

The term polymorphism refers to presence of many forms. Polymorphism, in other words, is the ability of a message to be displayed in more than one form. In technical terms, polymorphism refers to the usage of the same method name (but distinct signatures) for multiple types. A lady, for example, might have many characteristics at the same time, for example, a mother, wife, sister, employee, and so forth. As a result, the same individual exhibits diverse behavior in different settings. This is known as polymorphism.

We cannot create polymorphism in Go using classes since Go does not allow classes, but we can achieve it using interfaces. As previously stated, interfaces are implicitly implemented in Go. So, when we establish an interface and other kinds want to implement it, those types utilize the interface with the aid of the interface's methods without knowing the type. A variable of an interface type in an interface can hold any value that implements the interface. In the Go programming language, this characteristic aids interfaces in achieving polymorphism. Let us use an example.

```
// Program to illustrate the
// concept of polymorphism using the interfaces
package main
import "fmt"
```

```go
// Interface
type employee interface {
    develop() int
    name() string
}
// Structure1
type team1 struct {
    totalapp_1 int
    name_1      string
}
// Methods of employee interface
// are implemented by team1 structure
func (tm1 team1) develop() int {
    return tm1.totalapp_1
}
func (tm1 team1) name() string {
    return tm1.name_1
}
// Structure 2
type team2 struct {
    totalapp_2 int
    name_2      string
}
// Methods of the employee interface are
// implemented by team2 structure
func (tm2 team2) develop() int {
    return tm2.totalapp_2
}
func (tm2 team2) name() string {
    return tm2.name_2
}
func finaldevelop(i []employee) {
    totalproject := 0
    for _, ele := range i {
        fmt.Printf("\nThe Project environment = %s\n
", ele.name())
        fmt.Printf("The Total number of project %d\n
", ele.develop())
        totalproject += ele.develop()
    }
    fmt.Printf("\nThe Total projects completed by "+
        "the company = %d", totalproject)
}
```

```
// The main function
func main() {
    res1 := team1{totalapp_1: 20,
        name_1: "IOS"}
    res2 := team2{totalapp_2: 35,
        name_2: "Android"}
    final := []employee{res1, res2}
    finaldevelop(final)
}
```

Explanation: In the above example, an interface name is used as an employee. This interface has two methods: develop() and name(). The develop() method returns the total number of projects, while the name() method returns the name of environment in which they are created.

We now have two structures, team1 and team2. totalapp_1 int, name_1 string, totalapp_2 int, and name_2 string are the fields in both structures. These structures (team1 and team2) are now implementing the employee interface methods.

Following that, we write a finaldevelop() method that returns the total number of projects created by the organization. It takes an argument of a slice of employee interfaces. It estimates the total number of projects generated by the firm by iterating through the slice and calling the develop() function on each of its members. It also shows the project's environment by invoking the name() function. Different develop() and name() methods will be invoked depending on the concrete type of the employee interface. So, we accomplished polymorphism in the finaldevelop() method.

If you add another team to this program that implements an employee interface, the finaldevelop() function will determine the total number of projects created by the firm without regard for polymorphism.

This chapter covered structs definition, declaration of struct, nested and anonymous structure. We also covered method with the struct and non-type receiver. Moreover, we learned about interfaces, polymorphism, and inheritance.

CHAPTER 10

Concurrency and Goroutines

IN THIS CHAPTER

➤ Goroutines

➤ Channels

In Chapter 9, we discussed structs and interfaces. In this chapter, we will cover Goroutines and channels.

GOROUTINES – CONCURRENCY IN GoLang

A Goroutine is a particular feature of the Go programming language. A Goroutine is function or method that runs independently and concurrently with other Goroutines in our program. In other words, any continuously performing action in the Go programming language is referred to as a Goroutine. A Goroutine may be thought of as a lightweight thread. When compared to the thread, the cost of establishing Goroutines is quite low. Every program comprises at least one Goroutine, which is referred to as the main Goroutine. All of the Goroutines are subordinate to the main Goroutines; if the main Goroutine terminates, all of the goroutines in the program end. Goroutine is always working in the background.

Concurrency improves performance by utilizing many processing cores. Go's API support enables programmers to implement parallel algorithms

DOI: 10.1201/9781003310457-10

efficiently. Concurrency support is an optional feature in most major programming languages; however, it is built into Go.

Go Concurrent Programming

Concurrent programming makes full use of the numerous processor cores found in most contemporary systems. The notion has been around for a long time, even when the single core just had one core. Using several threads to create some form of concurrency was a widespread approach in many programming languages, including C/C++, Java, and others.

A single thread is essentially a small set of instructions scheduled to be executed individually. We might think of it as a small task within a larger project.

As a result, numerous threads of execution are combined and run concurrently to task a complicated process. This coherence across numerous jobs offers the impression of concurrent execution. However, keep in mind that any underlying constrained hardware – such as a single Processor – can only achieve so much by scheduling activities in a time-shared manner.

Multiple cores power today's computing devices. As a result, a language that can fully use its potential is constantly in demand. Mainstream programming languages progressively recognize this truth and attempt to include concurrency into their primary capabilities. However, the Go creators reasoned, "Why not construct a language from the ground up with the concept of concurrency as one of its basic features?" One such language that provides high-level APIs for writing concurrent programs in Go.

Issues with Multithreading

Multithreaded applications are not only challenging to create and maintain but also to debug. Furthermore, breaking up any process using several threads is not always possible to make it as performant as concurrent programming. Multithreading has its own set of costs. The environment handles many tasks, including inter-process communication and shared memory access. The developers are allowed to concentrate on the task at hand rather than become entangled in parallel processing details.

Keeping these issues in mind, another option is to depend entirely on the operating system for multiprocessing. In this instance, it is the developer's job to handle the complexities of interprocess communication or the cost of shared-memory concurrency. This strategy is very tweakable in favor of performance, but it is also easy to mess up.

Concurrent Programming in Go

Go provides a threefold solution for concurrent programming.

- High-level support makes concurrency not only easier to implement but also easier to manage.

- Goroutines are used. Threads are heavier than goroutines.

- Without the intervention of developers, Go's automated garbage collection solves the complexity of memory management.

How to Handle Concurrency Issues in Go

The goroutines make it simple to build concurrency and fundamental primitives. The executing activity is referred to as a goroutine in this context. Consider a program having two functions that do not communicate with one another. In sequential execution, one function completes its execution before another is invoked. However, in Go, the function can be both active and executing simultaneously. This is simple if the functions are unconnected, but complications might arise when they are interconnected and share execution durations. Even with Go's high-level concurrency support, these problems cannot be avoided entirely, especially if the main function accomplishes its execution before the functions that rely on it. As a result, we must be cautious about making the main goroutine wait until all tasks have been performed.

Another issue is deadlock, which occurs when more than one goroutine locks a certain resource to retain exclusivity while another tries to acquire the same lock at the same time. This sort of danger is typical in concurrent programming, but Go includes a fix that eliminates the need for locks by utilizing channels. As the job is completed, a channel is often formed to notify the completion of execution. Another option is to use sync to wait for the report. WaitGroup. However, deadlock can still occur in any instance and, at most, can be prevented with careful design. Go simply offers the tools to plan the proper operation of concurrency.

Goroutine with WaitGroup Example

We may establish a goroutine by prefixing any function call with the term go. The function then acts as a thread by constructing a goroutine containing the call frame and scheduling it to operate as a thread. It can access any arguments, globals, or anything available within its reach, just like any other function.

Here is a basic code that may use to determine whether a website is up or down. The identical code is then applied to goroutine. Make a note of how the execution speed increases when we use concurrency.

```go
package main
import (
    "fmt"
    "net/http"
    "time"
)
func main() {
    start := time.Now()
    sitelist := []string{
        "https://www.google.com//",
        "https://www.youtube.com/",
        "https://www.pinterest.com/",
        "https://www.codeguru.com/",
        "https://www.nasa.gov/",
    }
    for _, site := range sitelist {
        GetSiteStatus(site)
    }
    fmt.Printf("\n\nTime elapsed since %v\n\n", time.
Since(start))

}
func GetSiteStatus(site string) {
    if _, err := http.Get(site); err != nil {
        fmt.Printf("%s is down\n", site)
    } else {
        fmt.Printf("%s is up\n", site)
    }
}
```

How to Create a Goroutine

We may simply create our own Goroutine by prefixing the function or method call with the go keyword, as seen in the following syntax:

Syntax:

```go
func name(){
// statement
}
```

```
// using go keyword as
// the prefix of our function call
go name()
```

Example:

```
// Program to illustrate the
// concept of Goroutine
package main
import "fmt"
func display(str string) {
    for c := 0; c < 5; c++ {
        fmt.Println(str)
    }
}
func main() {
    // Calling the Goroutine
    go display("Welcome")
    // Calling the  normal function
    display("Helloeveryone")
}
```

In the above example, we define a display() method and then call it in two distinct ways. The first is a Goroutine, such as go display("Welcome"), while the second is a normal function, such as display("Helloeveryone"). However, there is a problem: it only shows the result of the normal function, not the result of the Goroutine, since when a new Goroutine is called, Goroutine calls the returns immediately. The control does not wait for Goroutine to finish its execution; instead, it moves on to the next line following the Goroutine call and disregards the value provided by the Goroutine. So, to properly run a Goroutine, we made the following changes to our program:

Updated example:

```
// program to illustrate concept of Goroutine
package main

import (
    "fmt"
    "time"
)
```

```
func display(str string) {
    for w := 0; w < 5; w++ {
        time.Sleep(1 * time.Second)
        fmt.Println(str)
    }
}
func main() {
    // Calling Goroutine
    go display("Hello")
    // Calling the normal function
    display("Helloeveryone")
}
```

In our application, we introduced the Sleep() function, which causes the main Goroutine to sleep for 1 second in between 1-second the new Goroutine executes, shows "Hello" on the screen, and then terminates after 1-second the main Goroutine reschedules and does its action. This procedure continues until the value of z<5 is reached, at which point the main Goroutine ends. In this case, both the Goroutine and the normal function are able to function efficiently.

Goroutines provide the following advantages:

- Goroutines are less expensive than threads.

- Goroutines are stored on the stack, and the size of the stack can expand and shrink according to the program's needs. However, the size of the stack in threads is fixed.

- Goroutines can interact over the channel, and these channels are specifically intended to prevent race problems when using Goroutines to access shared memory.

- Assume a program has a single thread with several Goroutines attached to it. If any of the Goroutines blocks the thread owing to resource constraints, all of the remaining Goroutines will be assigned to a newly generated OS thread. The programmers are not aware of any of this information.

Anonymous Goroutines
In Go, we can start a Goroutine for an anonymous function, or in other words, we can construct an anonymous Goroutine simply by

using the go keyword as a prefix to that function, as seen in the following syntax:

Syntax:

```
// the Anonymous function call
go func (parameterlist){
// statement..
}(arguments)
```

Example:

```
// Program to illustrate how
// to create anonymous Goroutine
package main
import (
    "fmt"
    "time"
)
// the main function
func main() {

    fmt.Println("Welcome to the main function")
    // Creating the Anonymous Goroutine
    go func() {
        fmt.Println("Welcome to ourworld")
    }()
    time.Sleep(1 * time.Second)
    fmt.Println("GoodBye ")

}
```

SELECT STATEMENT

The select statement in Go is similar to the switch statement; however, the case statement in the select statement relates to communication, i.e., sent or received operation on the channel.

Syntax:

```
select{
case SendOrReceive1: // Statement..
case SendOrReceive2: // Statement..
case SendOrReceive3: // Statement..

.

.

default: // Statement..
```

Points to consider:

- For some circumstances, the select statement waits until the communication (send or receive operation) is ready before proceeding.

Example:

```
// Program to illustrate
// the concept of select statement
package main
   import("fmt"
 "time")
    // function 1
    func portal1(channel1 chan string) {
        time.Sleep(3*time.Second)
        channel1 <- "Welcome to channel1"
    }
    // function 2
     func portal2(channel2 chan string) {
        time.Sleep(9*time.Second)
        channel2 <- "Welcome to channel2"
     }
// the main function
func main(){
    // Creating the channels
    R1:= make(chan string)
    R2:= make(chan string)
    // calling function 1
    // and function 2 in the goroutine
    go portal1(R1)
    go portal2(R2)
    select{
        // case 1 for portal1
        case op1:= <- R1:
        fmt.Println(op1)
        // case 2 for portal2
        case op2:= <- R2:
        fmt.Println(op2)
    }
}
```

Explanation: In the preceding program, portal1 sleeps for 3 seconds, and portal2 sleeps for 9 seconds before starting. Now, choose statement waits till their sleep time is up, then selects case 2 and outputs "Welcome to channel1." If portal1 wakes up before portal2, the output will be "welcome to channel2."

- If select statement does not include a case statement, it will wait indefinitely.

Syntax:

```
select{}
```

Example:

```
// Program to illustrate
// the concept of select statement
package main
// the main function
func main() {
    // Select statement without any case
    select{ }
}
```

- The select statement's default statement is used to prevent the select statement from blocking. This statement is executed when there is no case statement, and the statement is ready to proceed.

Example:

```
// Program to illustrate
// the concept of select statement
package main
import "fmt"
// the main function
func main() {
    // the creating channel
    mychannel:= make(chan int)
    select{
      case <- mychannel:
      default:fmt.Println("Not-found")
}
}
```

- When no case statement is ready, and the select statement does not contain any default statements, the select statement will block until at least one case statement or communication can proceed.

Example:

```
// Program to illustrate
// the concept of select statement
package main
// the main function
func main() {
    // creating the channel
    mychannel := make(chan int)
    // channel is not ready and
    // no default case
    select{
        case <- mychannel:
    }
}
```

- If numerous cases are ready to proceed, one can select at random in the select statement.

Example:

```
// Program to illustrate
// the concept of select statement
package main
import "fmt"
    // function 1
    func portal1(channel1 chan string){
        for i := 0; i <= 4; i++{
            channel1 <- "Welcome to channel1"
        }
    }
    // function 2
    func portal2(channel2 chan string){
        channel2 <- "Welcome to channel2"
    }
// the main function
func main() {
    // Creating the channels
```

```
R1:= make(chan string)
R2:= make(chan string)

// calling the function 1 and function 2 in
goroutine
go portal1(R1)
go portal2(R2)
// the choice of selection of case is random
select{
    case op1:= <- R1:
    fmt.Println(op1)
    case op2:= <- R2:
    fmt.Println(op2)
}
}
```

MULTIPLE GOROUTINES

A Goroutine is a function or method in our program that runs independently and concurrently with other Goroutines. In other words, any concurrently performing action in the Go programming language is referred to as a Goroutine. We may have several goroutines in a single program in the Go programming language. We may easily construct a goroutine by prefixing the function or method call with the go keyword, as illustrated in the following syntax:

```
func name() {
// statement(s)
}
// using go keyword as
// the prefix of your function call
go name()
```

With the help of an example, we will now explore how to create and work on several goroutines:

```
// Program to illustrate the Multiple Goroutines
package main
import (
    "fmt"
    "time"
)
```

```go
// For goroutine 1
func Aname() {
    arr1 := [4]string{"Ronik", "Sunita", "Arman",
"Tia"}
    for tk1 := 0; tk1 <= 3; tk1++ {
        time.Sleep(150 * time.Millisecond)
        fmt.Printf("%s\n", arr1[tk1])
    }
}
// For goroutine 2
func Aid() {
    arr2 := [4]int{400, 201, 402, 203}
    for tk2 := 0; tk2 <= 3; tk2++ {
        time.Sleep(500 * time.Millisecond)
        fmt.Printf("%d\n", arr2[tk2])
    }
}
// the main function
func main() {
    fmt.Println("!The Main Go-routine Start!")
    // calling Goroutine 1
    go Aname()

    // calling Goroutine 2
    go Aid()
    time.Sleep(2900 * time.Millisecond)
    fmt.Println("\n! The Main Go-routine End!")
}
```

1. **Creation:** From the above example, we have two goroutines and the main goroutine, namely Aname and Aid. Here, Aname prints the authors' names, and Aid prints the authors' id.

2. **Working:** We have two goroutines, Aname and Aid, and one main goroutine here. When we run this program, the main goroutine starts, and prints "!The Main Go-routine Start!" Because the main goroutine is like a parent and the other goroutines are its children, the main goroutine runs first, followed by the other goroutines, and if the main goroutine terminates, the other goroutines terminate as well. As a result, following the main goroutine, the Aname and Aid goroutines begin functioning concurrently.

GoLang CHANNEL

A channel in Go is a medium via which a goroutine communicates with another goroutine in a lock-free manner. In other terms, a channel is a mechanism that allows one goroutine to transfer data to another. The channel is bidirectional by default, which implies that goroutines can transmit and receive data over the same channel, as illustrated in the following figure.

Channel

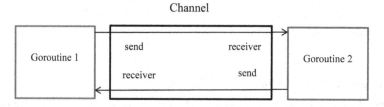

Channel in GoLang.

Creating a Channel

A channel is formed in Go using the chan keyword, and it can only transfer data of the same kind; multiple types of data cannot be sent from the same channel.

Syntax:

```
var Channelname chan Type
```

We may also use a shorthand declaration to build a channel with the make() method.

Syntax:

```
channelname := make(chan Type)
```

Example:

```
// Program to illustrate
// how to create channel
package main
import "fmt"
func main() {
    // Creating channel
    // Using the var keyword
    var mychannel chan int
```

```
    fmt.Println("The Value of the channel: ",
mychannel)
    fmt.Printf("The Type of the channel: %T ",
mychannel)
    // Creating channel using the make() function
    mychannel1 := make(chan int)
    fmt.Println("\nThe Value of the channel1: ",
mychannel1)
    fmt.Printf("The Type of the channel1: %T ",
mychannel1)
}
```

Send and Receive Data from a Channel

In the Go programming language, channels perform two primary operations: sending and receiving, collectively referred to as communication. And whether the data is received or sent is indicated by the direction of the <- operator. By default, the send and receive operations in the channel is blocked until the other side is ready. It enables goroutines to communicate with one another without explicit locks or condition variables.

Send Operation

The send operation sends data from one goroutine to another over a channel. Values, such as int, float64, and bool, are safe and simple to send across a channel because they are copied, eliminating the possibility of accidental concurrent access to the same value. Strings are similarly safe to transmit since they are immutable. However, transmitting pointers or references such as a slice, map, etc., across a channel is not safe since the value of the pointers or references may change by the sending or receiving goroutine at the same time, resulting in an unpredictable consequence. As a result, when using pointers or references in the channel, we must ensure that they can only access by one goroutine at a time.

```
Mychannel <- element
```

The above sentence indicates that the data(element) was sent to the channel(Mychannel) using the <- operator.

Receive Operation

The receive operation is used to receive data that sent by the send operator.

```
element := <-Mychannel
```

According to the above sentence, the element gets data from the channel (Mychannel). If the outcome of the received statement is not going to be used, the statement is also valid. A receive statement can alternatively write as:

```
<-Mychannel
```

Example:

```
// Program to illustrate send and
// receive operation
package main
import "fmt"
func myfunc(ch chan int) {
    fmt.Println(234 + <-ch)
}
func main() {
    fmt.Println("Main method start")
    // Creating channel
    ch := make(chan int)
    go myfunc(ch)
    ch <- 23
    fmt.Println("Main method end")
}
```

Channel Closing

We may also use the close() method to close a channel. This built-in function sets a flag indicating that no additional data will send to this channel.

Syntax:

```
close()
```

We may also use for range loop to close the channel. The receiver goroutine can use the following syntax to determine if the channel is open or closed:

Syntax:

```
ele, ok:= <- Mychannel
```

If the value of ok is true, this indicates that the channel is open and read operations can conduct. And if the value is false, it signifies that the channel is closed; therefore, read operations will fail.

Example:

```
// program to illustrate
// how to close channel using
// for range loop and close function
package main
import "fmt"
// Function
func myfun(mychnl chan string) {
    for k := 0; k < 4; k++ {
        mychnl <- "Helloeveryone"
    }
    close(mychnl)
}
// the main function
func main() {
    // Creating channel
    ch := make(chan string)
    // calling Goroutine
    go myfun(ch)
    // When value of ok is
    // set to true means
    // channel is open and
    // it can send or receive data
    // When value of ok is set to
    // false means channel is closed
    for {
        rest, ok := <-c
        if ok == false {
            fmt.Println("Channel-Close ", ok)
            break
        }
        fmt.Println("Channel-Open ", rest, ok)
    }
}
```

Important Notes:

- **Send and Receive Blocking:** When data is transferred to a channel, control is blocked in that send statement until another goroutine reads from that channel. Similarly, when a channel gets data from a goroutine, the read command is blocked until another goroutine statement is executed.

- **Channel with Zero Value:** The channel's zero value is nil.

- **For the Channel Loop:** A for loop can traverse over the values sent on the channel until it closes.

Syntax:

```
for item := range Chnl {
    // statement(s)
}
```

Example:

```
// Program to illustrate how
// to use for loop in the channel
package main
import "fmt"

// the main function
func main() {
    // Creating channel
    // Using the make() function
    mychnl := make(chan string)
    // Anonymous goroutine
    go func() {
        mychnl <- "HFE"
        mychnl <- "hfe"
        mychnl <- "hello"
        mychnl <- "Hellofromeveryone"
        close(mychnl)
    }()
    // Using the for loop
    for rest := range mychnl {
        fmt.Println(rest)
    }
}
```

- **Length of the Channel:** The length of the channel may be found in the channel by utilizing the len() method. The length, in this case, indicates the number of values queued in the channel buffer.

Example:

```
// Program to illustrate how to
// find the length of channel
package main
import "fmt"
// the main function
func main() {
     // Creating channel
    // Using the make() function
    mychnl := make(chan string, 4)
    mychnl <- "HFE"
    mychnl <- "hfe"
    mychnl <- "Hello"
    mychnl <- "Hellofromeveryone"
      // Finding length of the channel
    // Using the len() function
    fmt.Println("The Length of channel is: ",
len(mychnl))
}
```

- **Capacity of the Channel:** The cap() function in channel may be used to determine the channel's capacity. The capacity specifies the size of the buffer in this case.

Example:

```
// Program to illustrate
// how to find the capacity of the channel
package main
import "fmt"
// the main function
func main() {
    // Creating channel
    // Using the make() function
    mychnl := make(chan string, 5)
    mychnl <- "HFE"
    mychnl <- "hfe"
    mychnl <- "Geeks"
    mychnl <- "Helloeveryone"
    // Finding the capacity of channel
    // Using the cap() function
```

```
    fmt.Println("The Capacity of the channel is:
", cap(mychnl))
}
```

- **Select and Case Statement in the Channel:** A select statement in Go is similar to a switch statement in that it does not take any input parameters. This pick statement is used in the channel to perform a single operation from the case block's list of numerous operations.

UNIDIRECTIONAL CHANNEL

A channel, as we know, is a mechanism of communication between concurrently executing goroutines that allows them to send and receive data from each other. A bidirectional channel by default, but we may also construct a unidirectional channel. The unidirectional channel can only receive data or one that can only send data. The make() method can also use to construct a unidirectional channel, as demonstrated below:

```
// Only to receive the data
c1:= make(<- chan bool)
// Only to send the data
c2:= make(chan<-bool)
```

Example:

```
// Program to illustrate concept
// of unidirectional channel
package main
import "fmt"

// the main function
func main() {
    // Only for receiving
    mychanl1 := make(<-chan string)
    // Only for sending
    mychanl2 := make(chan<- string)
    // Display types of channels
    fmt.Printf("%T", mychanl1)
    fmt.Printf("\n%T", mychanl2)
}
```

Converting a Bidirectional Channel to a Unidirectional Channel

In Go, we may convert a bidirectional channel to a unidirectional channel, or in other words, a bidirectional channel to a receive-only or send-only channel, but not vice versa. It is shown in the following program:

Example:

```
// Program to illustrate how to
// convert bidirectional channel into
// the unidirectional channel
package main
import "fmt"
func sending(s chan<- string) {
    s <- "Helloeveryone"
}
func main() {
    // Creating bidirectional channel
    mychanl := make(chan string)
      // Here, sending() function convert
    // bidirectional channel into send only channel
    go sending(mychanl)

    // Here, channel is sent
    // only inside goroutine
    // outside goroutine the
    // channel is bidirectional
    // So, it print Helloeveryone
    fmt.Println(<-mychanl)
}
```

Use of Unidirectional Channel: The unidirectional channel is used to offer type-safety to the program, resulting in fewer errors. We may use a unidirectional channel when we want to create a channel that can only send or receive data.

In this chapter, we covered Go concurrent programming, how to handle concurrency issues in Go, how to create a Goroutine and select statement. We also covered multiple Goroutines, and GoLang channel.

CHAPTER 11

Packages in GoLang

IN THIS CHAPTER

➢ Packages in GoLang

➢ Documentation

In Chapter 10, we covered Goroutines and Channels. This chapter will cover packages with the creation and their documentation.

PACKAGES IN GoLang

We'll examine packages in the Go programming language in this session. Writing maintainable and reusable code is critical while developing software applications. Through its package ecosystem, Go delivers modularity and code reusability. Go encourages us to create little pieces of software as packages and then use these small packages to compose our programs.

Workspace

Before we go into Go packages, let's talk about structure code in Workspace. Programs in Go are maintained in a directory structure known as a workspace. A workspace is nothing more than the root directory for our Go applications. At the root of a workspace, there are three subdirectories:

- **src:** This directory includes source files grouped as packages. Inside this directory, we will develop our Go programs.

- **pkg:** Go package objects are stored in this directory.

- **bin:** This directory contains programs that may execute.

DOI: 10.1201/9781003310457-11

Before we can start writing Go programs, we must first define the location of the workspace. GOPATH is an environment variable that specifies the location of Go workspaces.

Packages

In Go, source files are grouped into system folders called packages, allowing code reuse among Go programs. The Go package naming convention utilizes the name of the system directory where we keep our Go source files. The package name will be same for all source files included within that directory within a single folder. We create Go programs under the $GOPATH directory, where we organize source code files into packages as directories. All identifiers in Go packages are exported to other packages if the initial letter of the identifier name is uppercase.

If we begin the identifier name with a lowercase letter, the functions and types will not export to other packages.

Go's standard library includes a plethora of helpful packages to construct real-world applications. The standard library, for example, has a "net/http" package that may use to create online applications and web services. The standard library packages may find in the GOROOT directory's "pkg" subfolder. When you install Go, an environment variable called GOROOT is added to our system to designate the Go installation path. The Go developer community is ecstatic about the prospect of creating third-party Go packages. These third-party Go packages can use for developing Go apps.

Main Package

When we create reusable code, you will create a package as a shared library. However, while creating executable applications, we will utilize the package "main" to convert the package into an executable program. The package "main" instructs the Go compiler to construct the package as an executable application rather than a shared library. The main function in package "main" will serve as the executable program's entry point. When you create shared libraries, there will be no main package or main function in the package.

Here's an example executable program that uses the package main, with the function main serving as the entry point.

```
package main
import (
"fmt"
```

```
)
func main(){
  fmt.Println("Hello, Everyone")
}
```

Importing Packages

When importing a package into another package, "import" is used. We imported the package "fmt" into the sample program in Code to use the method Println. The "fmt" package is part of the Go standard library. When we import packages, the Go compiler searches for them in the locations indicated by the environment variables GOROOT and GOPATH. The GOROOT directory contains packages from the standard library. The GOPATH location contains packages that we have written and third-party packages that we have imported.

Installing Third-Party Packages

We may get and install third-party Go packages by using "Go get" command. The Go get command will retrieve the packages from the source repository and place them in the GOPATH location.

In the terminal, type following command to install "mgo," a third-party Go driver package for MongoDB, into our GOPATH, which may be used across all projects in the GOPATH directory:

```
go get gopkg.in/mgo.v2
```

After installing the mgo, add the following import statement to our apps to reuse the code:

```
import (
        "gopkg.in/mgo.v2"
        "gopkg.in/mgo.v2/bson"
)
```

The MongoDB driver, mgo, provides two packages we have imported in the preceding import statement.

Init Function

When writing Go packages, we may include a function called "init" that is called at the start of the execution period. The init function is useful for adding initialization logic into a package.

```
package db
import (
        "gopkg.in/mgo.v2"
        "gopkg.in/mgo.v2/bson"
)
func init {
   // here initialization-code
}
```

In some instances, we may need to import a package to invoke its init function, and we do not need to call any of the package's other methods. If we import a package but do not use the package identification in the program, the Go compiler will complain. In this case, we may use a blank identifier (_) as the package alias name. The compiler will overlook the mistake of not utilizing the package identifier while still invoking the init function.

```
package main
import (
        _ "mywebapp/libs/mongodb/db"
  "fmt"
  "log"
)
func main() {
  //implementation-here
}
```

We imported a package called db into the sample program above. Assume we want to utilize this package to call the init function. The blank identifier will dodge the Go compiler error and execute the init function specified in the package.

To avoid package name ambiguity, we can use alias names for packages.

```
package main
import (
        mongo "mywebapp/libs/mongodb/db"
        mysql "mywebapp/libs/mysql/db"
)
func main() {
    mongodata :=mongo.Get() //calling the method of
package  "mywebapp/libs/mongodb/db"
    sqldata:=mysql.Get() //calling the method of
package "mywebapp/libs/mysql/db"
```

```
     fmt.Println(mongodata )
     fmt.Println(sqldata )
}
```

We're importing two separate packages from two different locations, but their names are identical. We may create an alias name for a single package and use it anytime we need to invoke a method in that package.

Important Considerations

1. **Import Paths:** In the Go programming language, each package is specified by a unique string called an import path. We may import packages into our program using an import route. As an example:

```
import "fmt"
```

As stated in this sentence, we are importing fmt package into our program. Package import paths are unique on a global scale. To avoid conflicts with the paths of other packages than the standard library, the package path should begin with the Internet domain name of the entity that owns or hosts the package. As an example:

```
import "geeksforgeeks.com/example/strings"
```

2. **Package Declaration:** In the Go programming language, a package declaration is always included at the beginning of the source file. Its function is to set the default identifier for that package when another package imports it. As an example:

```
package main
```

3. **Import Declaration:** The import declaration follows the package declaration immediately. The Go source file has one or more import declarations, each of which gives the path to one or more packages in parentheses. As an example:

```
// Importing the single package
import "fmt"
// Importing the multiple packages
import(
"fmt"
"strings"
"bytes"
)
```

When we import a package into our program, we have access to the package's members. For example, we have a package called "sort," and we can access sort when we import it into our program. Sort, Float64s() That package's SearchStrings() and other functionalities.

4. **Blank Import:** In Go programming, there are occasions when we import certain packages but do not utilize them. When we execute programs that include unused packages, the compiler will generate an error. We use a blank identifier before the package name to circumvent this problem. As an example:

```
import _ "strings"
```

It's referred to as a blank import. It is used in several situations when the main program can enable the extra capabilities given by the blank importing additional packages at compile-time.

5. **Nested Packages:** In Go, we may construct a package within another package by simply establishing a subdirectory. And the nested package, like the root package, may import. As an example:

```
import "math/cmplx"
```

The math package is the primary package in this case, while the cmplx package is the nested package.

6. Although some packages may have the same name, the route to such packages is always distinct. For example, both the math and crypto packages have a rand-named package, but their paths are different, i.e., math/rand and crypto/rand.

7. In Go programming, why is the main package usually at the top of the program? Because the main package instructs the go build that the linker must enable to create an executable file.

Giving the Packages Names

When naming a package in Go, we must always keep the following criteria in mind:

- When constructing a package, we must keep the name brief and concise. Strings, time, flags, and so on are examples of standard library packages.

- The name of the package should be descriptive and clear.

- Always attempt to avoid using names already in use or those used for local relative variables.

- The package's name is usually written in the singular form. To prevent keyword conflicts, several packages are named in plural form, such as strings, bytes, buffers, and so on.

- Always avoid package names with pre-existing meanings.

Example:

```
// Program to illustrate
// the concept of packages
// Package declaration
package main
// Importing the multiple packages
import (
    "bytes"
    "fmt"
    "sort"
)
func main() {
    // Creating and initializing the slice
    // Using the shorthand declaration
    slice_1 := []byte{'*', 'H', 'e', 'l', 'l',
'o', 'f',
        'o', 'r', 'W', 'o', 'r', 'k', 's', '^', '^'}
    slice_2 := []string{"hel", "lo", "for", "wor",
"ks"}
    // Displaying the slices
    fmt.Println("Original-Slice:")
    fmt.Printf("Slice 1 : %s", slice_1)
    fmt.Println("\nSlice 2: ", slice_2)
    // Trimming the specified leading
    // and trailing Unicode points
    // from given slice of bytes
    // Using the Trim function
    res := bytes.Trim(slice_1, "*^")
    fmt.Printf("\nNew Slice : %s", res)
    // Sorting the slice 2
    // Using the Strings function
```

```
    sort.Strings(slice_2)
  fmt.Println("\nSorted slice:", slice_2)
}
```

Code Exported

We might have noticed the declarations in the greet.go file we called were all uppercase. Go, unlike other languages, does not have the idea of public, private, or protected modifiers. Capitalization governs external visibility. Types, variables, functions, and that begin with a capital letter are publicly accessible outside of the current package. A symbol that can be seen outside of its container is termed exported.

If we add a new reset method to Octopus, we may call it from the welcome package but not from our main.go file, which is not part of the greet package:

```
package greet
import "fmt"
var Shark = "Rammy"
type Octopus struct {
        Name   string
        Color string
}
func (o Octopus) String() string {
        return fmt.Sprintf("Octopus's name is %q and
the color %s.", o.Name, o.Color)
}
func (o *Octopus) reset() {
        o.Name = ""
        o.Color = ""
}
func Hello() {
        fmt.Println("Hello, Everyone")
}
```

If we attempt to call reset from the main.go ahead and file:

```
package main
import (
        "fmt"
        "github.com/gopherguides/greet"
)
```

```
func main() {
        greet.Hello()
        fmt.Println(greet.Shark)
        oct := greet.Octopus{
                Name:  "Tessa",
                Color: "White",
        }
        fmt.Println(oct.String())
        oct.reset()
}
```

We'll receive the compilation error.

To export Octopus' reset functionality, capitalize the R in reset:

```
package greet
import "fmt"
var Shark = "Rammy"
type Octopus struct {
        Name   string
        Color  string
}
func (o Octopus) String() string {
        return fmt.Sprintf("The octopus's name is %q
and is the color %s.", o.Name, o.Color)
}
func (o *Octopus) Reset() {
        o.Name = ""
        o.Color = ""
}
func Hello() {
        fmt.Println("Hello, Everyone")
}
```

As a consequence, we may use Reset from another package without seeing an error:

```
package main
import (
        "fmt"
        "github.com/gopherguides/greet"
)
```

```go
func main() {
        greet.Hello()
        fmt.Println(greet.Shark)
        oct := greet.Octopus{
                Name:  "Tessa",
                Color: "White",
        }
        fmt.Println(oct.String())
        oct.Reset()
        fmt.Println(oct.String())
}
```

Now if we run the program:

```
$ go run main.go
```

DOCUMENTATION

Go provides the ability to produce documentation for packages we develop comparable to regular package documentation. Run the following command in a terminal:

```
godoc golang-book/chapter11/math Average
```

We can enhance this documentation by including the following note before the function:

```go
// Finds the average of a series of numbers
func Average(xs []float64) float64 {
```

If we run go install in the math folder, then godoc, we should notice our remark underneath the function definition. This documentation is also available in online form if we perform the following command:

```
godoc -http=":6060"
```

and enter following URL into our browser:

```
http://localhost:6060/pkg/
```

We should go through all of the packages on our system.

In this chapter, we covered packages and their documentation.

CHAPTER 12

The Core Packages

IN THIS CHAPTER

➤ String

➤ Input/output

➤ Files and folders

➤ Errors

➤ Containers and sort

➤ Hashes and cryptography

➤ Servers

➤ Parsing command line arguments

➤ Synchronization primitives

In Chapter 11, we covered creating packages and documentation. This chapter will discuss strings, input/output, files and folders, and errors. We will also cover containers and sort, hashes and cryptography, servers, parsing command line arguments, and synchronization primitives.

Most real-world programming relies on our ability to integrate with existing libraries rather than writing everything from scratch. This chapter will go through some of the popular Go packages.

First, a word of caution: while some of these libraries are relatively obvious, many of the libraries bundled with Go need specialist subject expertise (for example, cryptography).

DOI: 10.1201/9781003310457-12

STRING

In the strings package, Strings Go contains a vast variety of functions for working with strings:

```go
package main
import (
  "fmt"
  "strings"
)
func main() {
  fmt.Println(
    // true
    strings.Contains("rest", "es"),
    // 2
    strings.Count("rest", "r"),
    // true
    strings.HasPrefix("rest", "re"),
    // true
    strings.HasSuffix("rest", "st"),
    // 1
    strings.Index("rest", "e"),
    // "x-y"
    strings.Join([]string{"x","y"}, "-"),
    // == "xxxxx"
    strings.Repeat("x", 5),
    // "yyxx"
    strings.Replace("xxxx", "x", "y", 2),
    // []string{"x","y","z","a","b"}
    strings.Split("x-y-z-a-b", "-"),
    // "rest"
    strings.ToLower("REST"),
    // "REST"
    strings.ToUpper("rest"),
  )
}
```

We occasionally need to work with strings as binary data. To convert a string to a byte slice, perform the following:

```go
arr := []byte("rest")
str := string([]byte{'r','e','s','t'})
```

INPUT/OUTPUT (I/O)

The io package contains a few functions, most of which are interfaces used by other packages. Reader and Writer are the two main interfaces. Readers help reading by using the Read method. Writers assist writers using the Write method. Many Go functions accept Readers or Writers as arguments. The io package, for example, includes a Copy function that transfers data from Reader to Writer:

```
func Copy(dst Writer, src Reader) (written int64, err
error)
```

The Buffer struct from the bytes package may use to read or write to a [] byte or a string:

```
var buf bytes.Buffer
buf.Write([]byte("test"))
```

A Buffer does not need to be initialized and may be used with the Reader and Writer interfaces. The buf can use to convert it into a []byte by calling bug.Bytes(). We may also utilize the strings if we need to read from a string.NewReader method is faster than using a buffer.

FILES AND FOLDERS

To open a file, use the os package's Open function. An example of how to read a file's contents and show them on the terminal:

```
package main

import (
  "fmt"
  "os"
)
func main() {
  file, err := os.Open("rest.txt")
  if err != nil {
    // handle error here
    return
  }
  defer file.Close()
  // get file size
  stat, err := file.Stat()
```

```
if err != nil {
  return
}
// read file
bs := make([]byte, stat.Size())
_, err = file.Read(bs)
if err != nil {
  return
}
str := string(bs)
fmt.Println(str)
}
```

We utilize a deferred file.Close() should be called immediately after opening the file to ensure it is closed as soon as the function is finished. Because reading files is so common, there is a quicker way to accomplish this:

```
package main
import (
  "fmt"
  "io/ioutil"
)
func main() {
  bs, err := ioutil.ReadFile("rest.txt")
  if err != nil {
    return
  }
  str := string(bs)
  fmt.Println(str)
}
```

Here's how we'd go about creating a file:

```
package main
import (
  "os"
)
func main() {
  file, err := os.Create("rest.txt")
  if err != nil {
    // handle error here
    return
  }
```

```
   defer file.Close()
   file.WriteString("rest")
}
```

To retrieve the contents of a directory, we use the same os.Open method, but we pass it a directory path rather than a file name this time. The Readdir method is then invoked:

```
package main
import (
   "fmt"
   "os"
)
func main() {
   dir, err := os.Open(".")
   if err != nil {
      return
   }
   defer dir.Close()
   fileInfos, err := dir.Readdir(-1)
   if err != nil {
      return
   }
   for _, fi := range fileInfos {
      fmt.Println(fi.Name())
   }
}
```

We often want to recursively walk a folder (read the folder's contents, all the sub-folders, all the sub-sub-folders,…). To help with this, the path/file-path package has a Walk function:

```
package main
import (
   "fmt"
   "os"
   "path/filepath"
)
func main() {
   filepath.Walk(".", func(path string, info
os.FileInfo, err error) error {
      fmt.Println(path)
```

```
    return nil
  })
}
```

The function calls every file and folder in the root folder we pass to Walk.

ERRORS

Go includes a built-in type for previously seen errors (the error type). Using the New function in errors package, we may build our own errors:

```
package main
import "errors"
func main() {
  err := errors.New("error-message")
}
```

CONTAINERS AND SORTING

Go's container package has a number of different collections in addition to lists and maps. As an example, consider the container/list package.

List

The list package implements doubly linked list. A linked list is a form of data structure that looks like this:

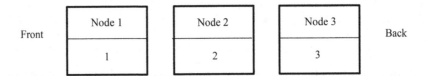

Linked list.

Each node in list has a value (1, 2, or 3 in this example) and a link to the next node. Because this is a doubly-linked list, each node has a pointer to the node before it. This program may generate the following list:

```
package main
import ("fmt" ; "container/list")
func main() {
  var y list.List
  y.PushBack(1)
  y.PushBack(2)
  y.PushBack(3)
```

```
for c := y.Front(); c != nil; c=c.Next() {
    fmt.Println(c.Value.(int))
  }
}
```

A List with a zero value is an empty list (*List may also be generated using list.New). PushBack is used to append values to the list. We loop over the list, starting with the first element and following all the connections until we reach nil.

SORT

Sorting arbitrary data is supported by the sort package. There are a variety of built-in sorting functions (for slices of ints and floats) Here's an example of how we can sort our data:

```
package main
import ("fmt" ; "sort")
type Person struct {
  Name string
  Age int
}
type ByName []Person
func (this ByName) Len() int {
  return len(this)
}
func (this ByName) Less(x, y int) bool {
  return this[x].Name < this[y].Name
}
func (this ByName) Swap(x, y int) {
  this[x], this[y] = this[y], this[x]
}

func main() {
  kids := []Person{
    {"Thill",7},
    {"Rach",11},
  }
  sort.Sort(ByName(kids))
  fmt.Println(kids)
}
```

The Sort function takes a sort. It is interfaced with and sorted. That sort. Interface necessitates three methods: Len, Less, and Swap. We build a new type (ByName) that relates to a slice of what we wish to sort to design our own sort. The three techniques are then defined.

Therefore, sorting our person list is as simple as casting the list into our new type. We may also order by age by doing the following:

```
type ByAge []Person
func (this ByAge) Len() int {
  return len(this)
}
func (this ByAge) Less(x, y int) bool {
  return this[x].Age < this[y].Age
}
func (this ByAge) Swap(x, y int) {
  this[x], this[y] = this[y], this[x]
}
```

HASHES AND CRYPTOGRAPHY

A hash function lowers a collection of data to a smaller fixed size. Hashes are often used in programming for various purposes ranging from data lookup to simply identifying changes. In Go, hash functions are classified as cryptographic or non-cryptographic.

Non-cryptographic hash functions include adler32, crc32, crc64, and fnv, which may be found in the hash package. Here's an example that makes use of crc32:

```
package main
import (
  "fmt"
  "hash/crc32"
)
func main() {
  x := crc32.NewIEEE()
  x.Write([]byte("rest"))
  y := h.Sum32()
  fmt.Println(y)
}
```

Because the crc32 hash object implements the Writer interface, we may write bytes to it the same way as any other Writer. After we've typed all we need, we'll call Sum32() to get an uint32. The comparison of two files is a popular use for crc32. If Sum32 value for both files is the same, it is extremely likely (but not definite) that the files are the same. If the values differ, the files are not the same:

```go
package main
import (
  "fmt"
  "hash/crc32"
  "io/ioutil"
)
func getHash(filename string) (uint32, error) {
  bs, err := ioutil.ReadFile(filename)
  if err != nil {
    return 0, err
  }
  x := crc32.NewIEEE()
  x.Write(bs)
  return x.Sum32(), nil
}
func main() {
  x1, err := getHash("rest1.txt")
  if err != nil {
    return
  }
  x2, err := getHash("rest2.txt")
  if err != nil {
    return
  }
  fmt.Println(x1, x2, x1 == x2)
}
```

Cryptographic hash functions are comparable to non-cryptographic hash functions, but they have the additional property of being difficult to reverse. It is complicated to establish who created a cryptographic hash of data collection. These hashes are frequently employed in security applications.

SHA-1 is known cryptographic hash function. Here's how it's put to use:

```go
package main
import (
  "fmt"
```

```
    "crypto/sha1"
)
func main() {
  x:= sha1.New()
  x.Write([]byte("rest"))
  bs := x.Sum([]byte{})
  fmt.Println(bs)
}
```

Because crc32 and sha1 both implement the hash.Hash interface, this example is quite identical to the crc32 one. The primary distinction is that, whereas crc32 generates a 32-bit hash, sha1 generates a 160-bit hash. Because there is no native type to represent a 160-bit integer, we use a 20-byte slice instead.

SERVERS

It is relatively simple to create network servers in Go. We'll start by looking at how to create a TCP server:

```
package main
import (
  "encoding/gob"
  "fmt"
  "net"
)
func server() {
  // listen on a port
  l, err := net.Listen("tcp", ":9999")
  if err != nil {
    fmt.Println(err)
    return
  }
  for {
    // accept a connection
    x, err := ln.Accept()
    if err != nil {
      fmt.Println(err)
      continue
    }
    // handle the connection
```

```go
      go handleServerConnection(x)
   }
}

func handleServerConnection(c net.Conn) {
   // receive message
   var msg string
   err := gob.NewDecoder(c).Decode(&msg)
   if err != nil {
      fmt.Println(err)
   } else {
      fmt.Println("Receive", msg)
   }
   x.Close()
}
func client() {
   // connect to the server
   x, err := net.Dial("tcp", "127.0.0.1:9999")
   if err != nil {
      fmt.Println(err)
      return
   }
   // send message
   msg := "Hello Everyone"
   fmt.Println("Sending", msg)
   err = gob.NewEncoder(x).Encode(msg)
   if err != nil {
      fmt.Println(err)
   }
   x.Close()
}
func main() {
   go server()
   go client()
   var input string
   fmt.Scanln(&input)
}
```

This example employs the encoding/gob package, which makes it simple to encode Go values so that other Go programs (or, in this case, the same Go program) can read them. Additional encodings can find in packages beneath encoding (such as encoding/json) and in third-party packages.

HTTP

HTTP servers are even simpler to set up and operate:

```
package main
import ("net/http" ; "io")
func helloo(res http.ResponseWriter, req *http.
Request) {
  res.Header().Set(
    "Content-Type",
    "text/html",
  )
  io.WriteString(
    res,
    '<DOCTYPE html>
<html>
  <head>
      <title>Hello Everyone</title>
  </head>
  <body>
      Hello Everyone!
  </body>
</html>',
  )
}
func main() {
  http.HandleFunc("/helloo", helloo)
  http.ListenAndServe(":9000", nil)
}
```

HandleFunc handles a URL route (/helloo) by calling the given function. We may also use FileServer to handle static files:

```
http.Handle(
  "/assets/",
  http.StripPrefix(
    "/assets/",
    http.FileServer(http.Dir("assets")),
  ),
)
```

RPC

The net/rpc and net/rpc/jsonrpc packages make it simple to provide methods for use over a network (rather than in the program that executes them).

```
package main
import (
  "fmt"
  "net"
  "net/rpc"
)
type Server struct {}
func (this *Server) Negate(i int64, reply *int64)
error {
  *reply = -i
  return nil
}
func server() {
  rpc.Register(new(Server))
  ln, err := net.Listen("tcp", ":9999")
  if err != nil {
    fmt.Println(err)
    return
  }
  for {
    x, err := ln.Accept()
    if err != nil {
      continue
    }
    go rpc.ServeConn(x)
  }
}
func client() {
  x, err := rpc.Dial("tcp", "127.0.0.1:9999")
  if err != nil {
    fmt.Println(err)
    return
  }
  var result int64
  err = x.Call("Server.Negate", int64(999), &result)
  if err != nil {
    fmt.Println(err)
```

```
    } else {
      fmt.Println("Server.Negate(999) =", result)
    }
}
func main() {
  go server()
  go client()
  var input string
  fmt.Scanln(&input)
}
```

This program is identical to the TCP example, except that now we've created an object to store all of the methods we want to expose, and we've called the Negate method from the client.

PARSING THE COMMAND LINE ARGUMENTS

When we run a command from the terminal, we may feed it arguments. We've seen this using the go command:

```
go run mytestfile.go
```

Arguments are run and mytestfile.go. We may also pass a command flags:

```
go run -v mytestfile.go
```

We may use the flag package to parse arguments and flags sent to our program. Here is a program that produces a number between 0 and 6. We may adjust the maximum value by sending a flag to the program (-max=100):

```
package main
import ("fmt";"flag";"math/rand")
func main() {
  // Define the flags
  maxp := flag.Int("max", 6, "max value")
  // Parse
  flag.Parse()
  // Generate a number between 0 and max
  fmt.Println(rand.Intn(*maxp))
}
```

flag.Args() returns a []string if there are any additional non-flag arguments.

SYNCHRONIZATION PRIMITIVES

The sync and sync/atomic packages in Go enable more typical multi-threading functions.

Mutexes

A mutex (mutal exclusive lock) is used to protect shared resources from non-atomic operations by locking a block of code to single thread at a time. A mutex is illustrated below:

```go
package main
import (
  "fmt"
  "sync"
  "time"
)
func main() {
  x := new(sync.Mutex)
  for c := 0; c < 10; c++ {
    go func(i int) {
      x.Lock()
      fmt.Println(c, "start")
      time.Sleep(time.Second)
      fmt.Println(c, "end")
      x.Unlock()
    }(i)
  }
  var input string
  fmt.Scanln(&input)
}
```

If the mutex (x) is locked, any further attempts to lock it will fail until it is unlocked. Extreme caution should be taken when utilizing mutexes or the synchronization primitives offered by the sync/atomic package.

Traditional multithreaded programming is challenging; mistakes are simple to make. Those problems are difficult to identify since they may depend on a highly specific, relatively rare, and difficult to duplicate set of circumstances. One of Go's main advantages is its concurrency capabilities are considerably easier to comprehend and apply than threads and locks.

In this chapter, we covered the core packages. We discussed strings, input/output, files and folders, errors, containers and sort, hashes and cryptography, servers, parsing command line arguments, and synchronization primitives.

Appraisal

Go is a computer language created in 2007 by Google's Rob Pike, Robert Griesemer, and Ken Thompson. It is a statically typed language with syntax comparable to C. It has garbage collection, type safety, dynamic typing, and many advanced built-in types, including variable-length arrays and key-value maps. It also has an extensive standard library, and allows concurrent programming. Go is a programming language introduced in November 2009 and utilized in some of Google's production systems.

Packages are used to design programs to manage dependencies efficiently. Go programming implementations use a typical compile and link model to build executable binaries.

BENEFITS AND DRAWBACKS OF PROGRAMMING IN Go

The Go programming language has seen an explosive rise in popularity in recent years. Every startup appears to be utilizing it for its backend systems. Developers are drawn to it for a variety of reasons.

Go Is Quick

Go is a lightning-fast programming language. It is compiled to machine code; it will automatically outperform interpreted or virtual runtime languages. Go applications also build quickly, and the final binary is tiny. Our API builds in seconds and generates an 11.5 MB executable file.

Simple to Understand

Go's grammar is short compared to other languages, making it simple to learn. We can remember most of it, so we don't need to spend much time digging stuff up. It's also quite clean and simple to read. Non-Go programmers, particularly those used to C-style syntax, can typically read a Go program and understand what's going on.

Static Typing

Go is a highly typed, statically typed programming language. Primitive types include int, byte, and string. Structs are another type of structure. Like any strongly typed language, the type system allows the compiler to catch entire classes of problems. Go includes built-in types for lists and maps that are simple to use.

Types of Interfaces

Interfaces exist in Go, and any struct can fulfill an interface by simply implementing its functions. This allows you to decouple the code's dependencies. The dependencies may then mock in tests. We can develop more modular, testable programming by utilizing interfaces. Go also features first-class functions, which allow us to create code more functionally.

Standard Library

Go comes with a decent standard library. It has useful built-in routines for dealing with primitive kinds. Packages exist that make it simple to set up a web server, manage I/O, interact with encryption, and manipulate raw data. The standard library's JSON serialization and deserialization are simple. We may give JSON field names directly next to struct fields using "tags."

Testing Assistance

The standard library includes testing support. There is no need for an additional dependence. If we have a code named example.go, put our tests in a file called thing test.go, and then execute "go test", these tests will be run quickly by Go.

Tools for Static Analysis

Static analysis tools for Go are plentiful and powerful. Gofmt, in particular, formats our code according to Go's recommended style. This can help normalize a lot of conflicting perspectives on a project and free up our team's time to focus on what the code is doing. We run gofmt, golint, and vet every build, and if any warnings are discovered, the build fails.

Garbage Collection

Go's memory management was designed to be simpler than the memory management in C and C++. Objects that are dynamically allocated are trash collected. Go makes utilizing pointers considerably safer because it does not enable pointer arithmetic. It also provides the option of using value types.

Easier Concurrency Model

While concurrent programming is never easy, Go makes it easier than other programming languages. It is incredibly straightforward to establish a lightweight thread known as a "goroutine" and communicate with it over a "channel." It is also possible to create more complicated patterns.

WHAT IS ITS NAME? IS IT Go OR GoLang?

We may hear the language referred to as both Go and GoLang, which might be confusing. That said, GoLang is simply another name for Go, maintaining the official name.

The word GoLang was derived from the domain name of the official Go website, golang.org. Which is very useful because "GoLang" is considerably more searchable on Google than "Go." As a result, it makes life simpler for individuals seeking knowledge about the programming language.

WHY WE SHOULD STUDY Go

Simple Learning Curve

Go is one of the most fundamental programming languages available. It is simple to learn, especially if we are already familiar with another programming language.

Many Go developers who are confident in their teaching talents claim that they can teach a complete newbie how to construct an app in only a few hours.

According to the 2020 StackOverflow Developer Survey, one of the key reasons Go rose from 10th to 5th most popular programming language is because of its simplicity.

Good Documentation and Active Community

Go offers comprehensive and easy-to-understand documentation. The documentation is available on the official website.

Aside from documentation, Go has a strong and active community behind it, so we can always obtain help if we get stuck.

Because the hashtag #golang is widely used on Twitter, we may tweet our query with the hashtag attached if we get stuck.

With Go, We Can Get a Lot Done

Go is a versatile programming language, which can be used for various tasks like web development, data science, cloud computing, and more.

If we want to work in cloud computing, we should learn Go since systems like Amazon Web Services, Kubernetes, and Google Cloud Platform (GCP) all support it.

Wages Are Attractive

With a median pay of $74,000, Go workers are the third-highest paid behind Perl and Scala, according to the 2020 StackOverflow Developer Survey.

This amount is likely to increase more as Go grows in popularity year after year and is in high demand. So, if we want to make more money, we should learn Go.

Bibliography

7 Types of Golang Operators – golangprograms.com. (n.d.). 7 Types of Golang Operators – Golangprograms.Com; www.golangprograms.com. Retrieved July 11, 2022, from https://www.golangprograms.com/go-language/operators.html

8 Key Reasons to Choose Go Programming Language for Cloud Infrastructure Projects | Xoriant. (n.d.). Xoriant; www.xoriant.com. Retrieved July 11, 2022, from https://www.xoriant.com/blog/product-engineering/go-programming-language-for-cloud-infrastructure-projects.html

A Golang Tutorial with Code Examples | Toptal. (n.d.). Toptal Engineering Blog; www.toptal.com. Retrieved July 11, 2022, from https://www.toptal.com/go/go-programming-a-step-by-step-introductory-tutorial

A Practical Guide to Interfaces in Go (Golang) – golangbot.com. (2020, March 1). Go Tutorial – Learn Go from the Basics with Code Examples; golangbot.com. https://golangbot.com/interfaces-part-1/

Bodnar, J. (2022, April 25). *Go variable – working with variables in Golang.* Go Variable – Working with Variables in Golang; zetcode.com. https://zetcode.com/golang/variable/

Chapter 4. Arrays, slices, and maps · Go in Action. (n.d.). Chapter 4. Arrays, Slices, and Maps · Go in Action; livebook.manning.com. Retrieved July 11, 2022, from https://livebook.manning.com/book/go-in-action/chapter-4/20

Concurrency in Go | Engineering Education (EngEd) Program | Section. (n.d.). Engineering Education (EngEd) Program | Section; www.section.io. Retrieved July 11, 2022, from https://www.section.io/engineering-education/concurrency-in-go/#:~:text=In%20Go%2C%20concurrency%20works%20through,alongside%20other%20code%20or%20programs

Create an empty file in Golang – golangprograms.com. (n.d.). Create an Empty File in Golang – Golangprograms.Com; www.golangprograms.com. Retrieved July 11, 2022, from https://www.golangprograms.com/create-an-empty-file.html

DASC, T. is. (2020, July 11). *Seven Golang Features you must know about | by This is DASC | Medium.* Medium; medium.com. https://medium.com/@thisisdasc/seven-golang-features-you-must-know-about-944485d413fe

Fadatare, R. (n.d.). *Go (Golang) Read and Write File Example Tutorial.* Go (Golang) Read and Write File Example Tutorial; www.javaguides.net. Retrieved July 11, 2022, from https://www.javaguides.net/2021/05/go-golang-read-and-write-file-example.html

Forbes, E. (n.d.). *Reading And Writing To Files in Go | TutorialEdge.net*. TutorialEdge; tutorialedge.net. Retrieved July 11, 2022, from https://tutorialedge.net/golang/reading-writing-files-in-go/

Getting started with Golang: A tutorial for beginners. (n.d.). Educative: Interactive Courses for Software Developers; www.educative.io. Retrieved July 11, 2022, from https://www.educative.io/blog/golang-tutorial

Go – Functions. (n.d.). Go – Functions; www.tutorialspoint.com. Retrieved July 11, 2022, from https://www.tutorialspoint.com/go/go_functions.htm

Go Basic Syntax Tutorial | KoderHQ. (n.d.). Go Basic Syntax Tutorial | KoderHQ; www.koderhq.com. Retrieved July 11, 2022, from https://www.koderhq.com/tutorial/go/syntax/

Go Packages (With Examples). (n.d.). Go Packages (With Examples); www.programiz.com. Retrieved July 11, 2022, from https://www.programiz.com/golang/packages

Go Programming Language (Introduction) – GeeksforGeeks. (2018, April 25). GeeksforGeeks; www.geeksforgeeks.org. https://www.geeksforgeeks.org/go-programming-language-introduction/

Go Syntax. (n.d.). Go Syntax; www.w3schools.com. Retrieved July 11, 2022, from https://www.w3schools.com/go/go_syntax.php

Go Variables and Constants. (n.d.). Go Variables and Constants; www.programiz.com. Retrieved July 11, 2022, from https://www.programiz.com/golang/variables-constants

Golang Maps – GeeksforGeeks. (2019, July 22). GeeksforGeeks; www.geeksforgeeks.org. https://www.geeksforgeeks.org/golang-maps/

Golang Tutorial: Learn Go Programming Language for Beginners. (2020, January 1). Guru99; www.guru99.com. https://www.guru99.com/google-go-tutorial.html

Guide on Go Programming Language. (2019, October 1). Appinventiv; appinventiv.com. https://appinventiv.com/blog/mini-guide-to-go-programming-language/

How to become a Golang developer: 6 step career guide. (n.d.). Educative: Interactive Courses for Software Developers; www.educative.io. Retrieved July 11, 2022, from https://www.educative.io/blog/become-golang-developer

How to Create an Empty File in Golang? – GeeksforGeeks. (2020, March 12). GeeksforGeeks; www.geeksforgeeks.org. https://www.geeksforgeeks.org/how-to-create-an-empty-file-in-golang/

How to Install Go on Windows? – GeeksforGeeks. (2019, June 28). GeeksforGeeks; www.geeksforgeeks.org. https://www.geeksforgeeks.org/how-to-install-go-on-windows/#:~:text=Downloading%20and%20Installing%20Go&text=Step%201%3A%20After%20downloading%2C%20unzip,you%20want%20to%20install%20this

Interfaces in Golang – GeeksforGeeks. (2019, August 16). GeeksforGeeks; www.geeksforgeeks.org. https://www.geeksforgeeks.org/interfaces-in-golang/

Introduction to Functions in Golang | CalliCoder. (2018, March 29). CalliCoder; www.callicoder.com. https://www.callicoder.com/golang-functions/

Is Golang the Future? (n.d.). Is Golang the Future?; www.linkedin.com. Retrieved July 11, 2022, from https://www.linkedin.com/pulse/golang-future-georgia-luxton#:~:text=According%20to%20positronx%2C%20No%20doubt,it%20is%20well%20worth%20learning

Keva Laya, S. E. (2022, February 7). *Is Golang Worth Learning*. Career Karma; careerkarma.com. https://careerkarma.com/blog/is-golang-worth-learning/#:~:text=Yes%2C%20Golang%20is%20still%20worth,the%20most%20loved%20languages%20list

Nagarajan, M. (2020, May 12). *Learning Go—Array, Slice, Map*. Medium; levelup.gitconnected.com. https://levelup.gitconnected.com/learning-go-array-slice-map-934eed320b1c

Nnakwue, A. (2022, January 14). *Exploring structs and interfaces in Go – LogRocket Blog*. LogRocket Blog; blog.logrocket.com. https://blog.logrocket.com/exploring-structs-interfaces-go/

Packages in Golang – GeeksforGeeks. (2019, October 25). GeeksforGeeks; www.geeksforgeeks.org. https://www.geeksforgeeks.org/packages-in-golang/#:~:text=Packages%20are%20the%20most%20powerful,of%20the%20other%20package%20programs

Parr, K. (2021, September 13). *How to use pointers in Go – LogRocket Blog*. LogRocket Blog; blog.logrocket.com. https://blog.logrocket.com/how-to-use-pointers-in-go/

Reasons Why Golang is Better than other Programming Languages? (2021, May 7). Supersourcing; supersourcing.com. https://supersourcing.com/blog/reasons-why-golang-is-better-than-other-programming-languages/#:~:text=Golang%20is%20better%20than%20other%20programming%20languages%2C%20therefore%20it%20reduces,to%20save%20time%20and%20resources

Structs in Go (Golang) | Detailed Tutorial with Examples | golangbot.com. (2020, May 1). Go Tutorial – Learn Go from the Basics with Code Examples; golangbot.com. https://golangbot.com/structs/

Talim, S. M. (2015, September 2). *What is the future for Go?*. *This year I had the privilege to… | by Satish Manohar Talim | Medium*. Medium; medium.com. https://medium.com/@IndianGuru/what-is-the-future-for-go-e002b06a240b#:~:text=Baron%20Schwartz%20%E2%80%94%20Go%20programmers%20are,This%20will%20only%20increase

Top 7 Reasons to Learn Golang – GeeksforGeeks. (2020, August 16). GeeksforGeeks; www.geeksforgeeks.org. https://www.geeksforgeeks.org/top-7-reasons-to-learn-golang/#:~:text=Easy%20to%20Learn,to%20get%20the%20task%20done

Tutu, A. (2017, February 7). *Writing Your First Program with Go | by AnnMargaret Tutu | Medium*. Medium; codeamt.medium.com. https://codeamt.medium.com/writing-your-first-program-with-go-79ee6a3c3b4d

Understanding Control Structures in Go | Developer.com. (2021, November 25). Developer.Com; www.developer.com. https://www.developer.com/languages/control-structures-golang/

Understanding Pointers in Go | DigitalOcean. (2020, July 21). Understanding Pointers in Go | DigitalOcean; www.digitalocean.com. https://www.digital-ocean.com/community/conceptual_articles/understanding-pointers-in-go

What is the Go Programming Language? (2020, May 1). SearchITOperations; www.techtarget.com. https://www.techtarget.com/searchitoperations/definition/Go-programming-language#:~:text=Go%20(also%20called%20Golang%20or,is%20statically%20typed%20and%20explicit

Your First Program — An Introduction to Programming in Go | Go Resources. (n.d.). Your First Program — An Introduction to Programming in Go | Go Resources; www.golang-book.com. Retrieved July 11, 2022, from https://www.golang-book.com/books/intro/2

Index

Printed in the United States
by Baker & Taylor Publisher Services